About the Author

P9-APM-442

B orn in Tracadie, Nova Scotia, in 1884, Mary Loretta Gerin was educated in the province and then trained as a nurse at Boston City Hospital in 1910. She served briefly as a supervisor of nurses at the Boston Psychopathic Hospital before moving to Regina in 1914 with her husband, Melville Bell Weekes, a Saskatchewn civil servant. Weekes continued her professional career in Saskatchewan with the Victorian Order of Nurses, but soon gave up the work following the birth of the first of three sons. She turned her hand to writing short stories, first about nursing, then about the history of her adopted province. She developed a keen fascination for the prairies, which showed in her articles, short stories, and poetry, written for national and regional magazines. Her interview with Norbert Welsh in 1931 led to the book *The Last Buffalo Hunter* (1939), and her interview with William Cornwallis King in 1936 culminated in the book you are holding, *Trader King*. Weekes's other books include *Round Council Fires, Painted Arrows,* and *Great Chiefs and Mighty Hunters.* Mary Weekes died in 1980.

971.05092 King

King, W.
Trader King.

PRICE: $18.95 (3559/ex)

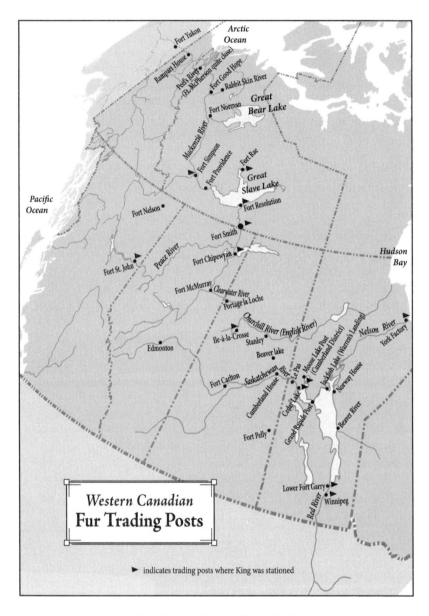

► indicates trading posts where King was stationed

Fur Trading Posts in Western and Northern Canada

Trader King

MARY WEEKES

As told to her by William Cornwallis King

The thrilling story of forty years' service in
the North-West Territories, related by one
of the last of the old-time wintering partners of the Hudson's Bay Company.

FIFTH
HOUSE

Copyright © 2007 Aileen Weekes
First published in 1949 by School Aids and Textbook Publishing Company, Ltd., Regina and Toronto

All rights reserved. No part of this publication may be reproduced, stored in a retrieval system, or transmitted, in any form or by any means, electronic, mechanical, recording, or otherwise, without the prior written permission of the publisher, except in the case of a reviewer, who may quote brief passages in a review to print in a magazine or newspaper, or broadcast on radio or television. In the case of photocopying or other reprographic copying, users must obtain a license from Access Copyright.

Cover and interior series design by Cheryl Peddie/Emerge Creative
Typesetting and cover work by Dean Pickup
Cover illustration of W. Cornwallis King by Kathleen Shackelton, 1937, courtesy Hudson's Bay Company Archives, Archives of Manitoba, HBCA P-273
Copyedited by Joan Tetrault
Proofread by Kirsten Craven
Map by Brian Smith/Articulate Eye

The publisher gratefully acknowledges the support of The Canada Council for the Arts and the Department of Canadian Heritage.

 Canada Council   Conseil des Arts
for the Arts   du Canada

We acknowledge the financial support of the Government of Canada through the Book Publishing Industry Development Program (BPIDP) for our publishing activities.

Printed in Canada

2007/1

First published in the United States in 2008 by
Fitzhenry & Whiteside
311 Washington Street
Brighton, Massachusetts 02135

Library and Archives Canada Cataloguing in Publication

King, William Cornwallis, 1845-1940
    Trader King / Mary Weekes ; as told to her by William Cornwallis King.

ISBN 978-1-897252-15-4

    1. King, William Cornwallis, 1845-1940. 2. Hudson's Bay Company–History.
3. Frontier and pioneer life–Canada, Northern. 4. Hudson's Bay Company–
Biography. 5. Fur traders–Canada–Biography. 6. Northwest, Canadian–
Biography. I. Weekes, Mary, 1884-1980 II. Title.

FC3217.1.K55A3 2007   971.05092   C2007-903125-0

Fifth House Ltd.
A Fitzhenry & Whiteside Company
1511, 1800-4 St. SW
Calgary, Alberta T2S 2S5

1-800-387-9776
www.fitzhenry.ca

Contents

Foreword

Chief Trader King, who died in 1940, was one of the most fearless and colourful traders of the Canadian North. From the day that he landed at York Factory in 1862 until his retirement from the Hudson's Bay Company in 1903 his life was filled with stirring adventure in a vast country where only skilled boatmen could make their way over the water routes from one post to the next and where only expert huntsmen and the most rugged individuals could survive. Through all his thousands of miles of travel and his responsibilities for precious cargo en route he had complete confidence in his own ability and that of the expert guides supplied by the Company, together with a sense of humour and a light heart, which tended to make each trip a glorious adventure rather than a test of endurance. He had a keen eye for business and from the first won the complete confidence of the Indians whom he in turn trusted and by whom he was seldom disappointed.

Mr. King's story is admirably written by Mrs. Mary Weekes, who obtained the data from Mr. King himself four years before his death. The use of the first person throughout makes the account realistic. The details relative to types of cargo, description of waterways, and the various kinds of fur-bearing animals supply for the student a veritable treasure chest of information on our own North and the manner in which it was first settled. It is a drama of amazing endurance and heroism and should appeal to teacher and pupil as not only fascinating reading but authentic discovery. The book is an excellent first-hand description of the conduct of business at the trading posts in the days of the fur trade during the last half of the nineteenth century.

H. Janzen,
Director of Curricula,
Dept. of Education, Regina

Our Multi-coloured Past

I n an article for *The Beaver* magazine of June 1935, celebrating
William Cornwallis King's ninetieth birthday, the editor, Douglas
MacKay, suggested that some day the fine old gentleman's
admirably clear memories of life in the fur trade would be gathered into
a book. This is the book. It was made possible by Mrs. Weekes's
patience and understanding, my husband's initiative and persuasion,
and Mr. King's collaboration in the final years of his long life.

These chapters are part of the tapestry of our Canadian story. It is
quite in character with our multi-coloured past that here the pattern
should be woven by an ardent young imperialist who was born in
India, educated in famous British schools, and spent the rest of his life
in the Canadian North-West, and also that the threads have been
neatly fastened by Nova Scotia-born, Boston-educated Mary Weekes,
who has lived longest in Regina, Saskatchewan. The fur-trading
described here is a peculiarly Canadian development, although few
fur traders from Groseilliers and Radisson down to recent years were
Canadian-born.

Mr. King was a lineal descendant of earlier fur trade giants. He
talked with an Indian who had guided Sir John Franklin. He knew Dr.
John Rae personally, and in his younger days in the Hudson's Bay
Company he heard echoes of battles with Northwesters and of the
rule of Sir George Simpson and the great John McLaughlin. Mr. King
was one of the last wintering partners of the Company, a survivor of
the time when chief factors and chief traders shared in the profits of
the "Company of Adventurers of England Trading into Hudson's Bay,"
and so were partners rather than salaried employees.

Although the rigid outlines of history must rest on a sound docu-
mentary basis, so long and vivid a memory as Mr. King's supplies a
wealth of detail seldom noted on official paper. Mr. King's mind was
uncluttered by anything outside the horizons of the ancient Company
which occupied his life. During his long years of quiet retirement his
memory remained bright, and for these pages he relived with keen
pleasure his young days in the old fur trade that has now gone forever.

ALICE MACKAY
Winnipeg, September 24, 1947

Preface

W illiam Cornwallis King was a handsome, erect figure of a man when the late Douglas Mackay (of the Hudson's Bay Company's Canadian committee executive) introduced us in 1935. Spare of frame, his white hair trim above a fine pair of deep blue eyes and a brief and tidy beard, he was one of those rare men who had grown old gently and gracefully. He accepted life as it came—even failing eyesight and the difficulty of hearing. He was living in a small, rented room with a kind-hearted family in Winnipeg, a room rather like Mr. King since it too was spare, clean, and neat. His mind was clear as a bell and he kept a bright sense of humour over, among other things, the fact that he had been on pension since 1903. He received visitors with complete and charming dignity, and the manners of an English gentleman of good family.

Mr. Mackay, who was then writing *The Honourable Company* and editing *The Beaver* magazine, had thoughtfully provided Hudson's Bay tobacco, and soon, his pipe properly alight, the old gentleman fell into pleasant reminiscence of Red River days and the Company, with which he had been identified as clerk, officer, and pensioner for more than three-quarters of a century.

We had many such sessions, until at times it seemed as if the clock had actually been turned back through the years. Inevitably we had to return to the present, and Mr. King expounded vigorously on the contrast with the more adventurous past.

"The spirit of Fort Garry is dead," he would say. "Traders, trappers, buffalo hunters, those magnificent voyageurs going up and down the rivers, the hunters creaking away from the trading post in their Red River carts, the drivers' voices as they shouted *marché* to the dog teams ... the natives singing, fighting—a hard-living, friendly lot ... the brides requisitioned by northern officers going off into the far country with the Red River brigade. That was the life of old Fort Garry. I remember when the first cat was brought in by an officer's wife."

Contemporary men, he thought, were less resourceful and venturesome than the comrades of frontier days. In the Company, also, they had lost the standing of partnership. He would often stop in his narrative to remark: "Madam, we *were* the Company," as indeed they were under the deed poll—a partnership contract which had its origin in the North West Company. It was abolished in 1869 when the Company surrendered its exclusive rights in Canada.

Sharply focused in the old officer's memory was the bitter rivalry that still existed, when he entered the Company, between the North West men who had been retained by the Hudson's Bay Company at the time of the amalgamation. He assured me: "The Northwesters had the brains. They were practical men—independent traders who had been in business for themselves and operating on their own capital. The Hudson's Bay officers had risen from positions of clerks to factors. When the Hudson's Bay Company had posts only on the Bay, the Northwesters were trading all over the country. *They* knew where to get furs."

The old officer found his deafness a great trial. He had an obsolete speaking tube upon which he depended a good deal, but, being extremely fastidious, when visitors shouted into the horn, as they often did, he was annoyed. He was surprised to discover that my voice had a carrying quality and delighted when I persuaded him that we could get on nicely without the objectionable tube.

In a great and contented way, Mr. King lived richly with his memories of early years. He would touch the Bible on his table and say, "My mother gave this to me when I left England and it has accompanied me in all my travels—across frozen wastes and through vicious rapids. No love in a man's life can replace the love he bears his mother. This Bible has been an inseparable link with my mother, God, and far-off England. And that plaid shawl on my bed draped my father's coffin. It came from India, as did this skull cap I wear, taken by my father off the head of a slain chieftain."

It was interesting to learn that the old officer had established trading posts for the Company in Mackenzie's river, as he called it, set up law and order in the vast lonely regions tributary to his posts, performed marriages, and buried the dead. To quote Mr. Douglas Mackay:

"Mr. King is one of the band of men who, living isolated in a great wilderness among Indians, never lost either their power to command or that sense of justice which enabled them to maintain the peace. One has only to look at the accounts of the opening up of other uncivilized areas of the world during the nineteenth century, with their records of savage warfare, to realize what men of the Company in the last century contributed to the history of the Canadian West. Mr. King's greatest pride is his years in the Northern Department, for the best in the service were sent to the Mackenzie River District. Discipline was strict and morale was high. There he lived, travelled, traded, took his years of furlough in England, and returned to the Company's service."

Lightened here and there by the old gentleman's keen sense of humour as his memory recalled old internal frictions within the Company, rivalries, challenges, and adventures, he plunged into his story.

Hudson's Bay London Archives supply the following history of Mr. King:

CHIEF TRADER WILLIAM CORNWALLIS KING

William Cornwallis King was born on April 6, 1845, and entered the service of the Hudson's Bay Company as an apprentice clerk in 1862. In his contract of service dated May 29, 1862, King is described as the son of Colonel Henry Cornwallis King of Oakley Cottage, Douglas, Isle of Man.

He sailed for York Factory on board the *Prince of Wales*—Captain D. J. Herd—and he apparently spent outfit 1862-63 at Lower Fort Garry, and in the following outfit he was transferred to Fort Resolution in the Mackenzie River District, where he remained until the end of outfit 1864-65.

In the autumn of 1865 it was decided to re-establish Fort Nelson on the Buffalo River—a tributary of the Liard River—and William Cornwallis King was supplied with an outfit for the post and instructed to erect temporary buildings, etc. In December

1865, Julian S. Onion (Julian S. Camsell as he was known later), clerk, was sent to take charge of this post and King was appointed his assistant. King apparently took charge of Fort Rae during outfit 1866-67 and he was promoted to the rank of clerk during outfit 1870-71, when he was granted furlough owing to the illness of his father.

On his return to North America in 1872 King proceeded to the Athabasca District, arriving at Fort Chipewyan on October 9. He served as clerk under Factor Roderick MacFarlane at this post until the end of outfit 1873-74, when he was appointed clerk in charge of Fort St. John for the ensuing season (1874-75).

He married Miss Charlotte Flett at Fort Chipewyan on August 4, 1874, by civil contract "in the presence of R. Macfarlane, J. P.," and a son was born to them at Fort Chipewyan on July 3 of the following year.

It has been difficult to trace King's movements during outfits 1875-76 and 1876-77, but he was probably stationed at Fort Chipewyan. From outfit 1877-78 until the end of outfit 1882-83 King was in charge of Fort Rae in the Mackenzie River District, and on July 13th, 1883, he assumed the charge of Fort Smith in the Athabasca District. During the early part of trading season 1884-85 King proceeded to England on furlough, but he returned to Canada in spring, 1885, and his services were used in the Clearwater River Scow Transport during the following summer. He was promoted to the rank of junior chief trader in 1884.

King was stationed at Ile-à-la-Crosse, under the charge of Chief Factor Joseph Fortescue, during the trading season 1885-86, and on June 17, 1886, Commissioner Joseph Wrigley instructed King to proceed to the charge of Fort Pelly in the Swan River District. He remained in charge of this post until the end of outfit 1888-89, when he proceeded to the charge of the posts at Moose Lake and Cedar Lake in the Cumberland District. During the following outfit (1890-91) it was considered advisable to make Cedar Lake the chief post and Moose Lake the outpost, so King accordingly moved his quarters to the former place some time during July 1890. He remained at Cedar Lake until the summer of 1893, when he went to England for a short furlough. He was back at his post by the early part of November 1893, and remained in charge there until July 1894. His next appointment was to the charge of the English River District at Ile-à-la-Crosse, and he apparently stayed there until the end of outfit 1898–99. He was promoted to the rank of chief trader on June 1, 1896.

During outfit 1899–1900 he is listed as a chief trader at the general office (Winnipeg) and he was in charge at York Factory during the following outfit (1900–1). He spent the winter of 1901–2 in the Keewatin District. This was his last winter of active service although his official retirement dates from June 1, 1903.

MARY WEEKES

I Join the "Company of Adventurers"

I was born in 1845 in the Neilghberry Hills, Madras Presidency, India, where my father, Colonel Henry Robert Cornwallis King, was a colonel of the Honourable East India Company, commanding the 6th Madras Light Cavalry.

In the year 1847, my brother, sister, and I were taken by my mother to England on the *Seringapatam*. My young sister died onboard ship. She was buried at sea. I am told that we were swung ashore in a basket chair from the ship on the East India Docks at Gravesend, England. These basket chairs held two people. They were lowered from the yardarm of the ship.

My mother left us in England, in charge of Dr. Edward Norton, the great liver pill man, in Upper Baker Street. For seven years we went to school in Herring Fleet Village, close to Great Yarmouth. This school was situated on property owned by Sir Robert Peto, the famous engineer and railroad man.

After a year at this school, my father retired from service in India and came to England, where he became colonel of the Bedfordshire Yeomanry. Later I was transferred to the Grammar (free) School, Bedford, and from there I went to the Blue Coat School, London. I attended King's College, in the Isle of Man from

1859-61. From King's College, in the spring of 1861, I went for six months to the Sandhurst Military College. When I went home for the holidays, I discovered that my father had set his heart on my entering the service of the East India Company. This was natural. The Company granted one military commission to each officer's son, military education being under their direction and at their expense. I held an officer's commission, ensign, when I was 17 years of age. Sandy McPherson, son of Chief Factor Cluny McPherson, of the Hudson's Bay Company in Canada, was in my dormitory at Sandhurst. He talked a great deal about his country and what he told me fired my imagination. He lent me a copy of Robert Ballantyne's book, *Hudson's Bay*. I was definitely committed to Canada.

My father was greatly disappointed when I refused to become an officer of the East India Company. He was opposed to my going into the Hudson's Bay Company[1] when I applied for a place in the service. I asked my cousins, Charles and Henry Barnett, London bankers for the East India Company and also the Hudson's Bay Company, to help me. They were influential enough to obtain for me the five-year apprentice clerk contract.

According to the custom of the Hudson's Bay Company, an annual dinner was held on the eve of the departure of the ships to Hudson's Bay. The governor of the London Board, the directors, the captain, and officers of the ship were there. I was required to attend. As luck would have it, I was the only apprentice clerk at this dinner; the others joined at Stromness. That day was a red-letter day in my life. The date was June 1, 1862; the ship *Prince of Wales*, Captain Herd, commanding officer. It was going to York Factory. Another ship, *Princess Royal*, in charge of Captain Royal, was there also on its way to Moose Factory.

Both ships left London on June 3. These were the only two vessels of the Company sailing to Hudson's Bay at this time. The morning of the great day arrived. We put out for Stromness in the Orkney Islands against headwinds. Our object in calling at Stromness was to take aboard supplies which had arrived too late to be taken on the ship before it left London, to pick up the engaged servants who were shipping aboard here, and to await final orders from Hudson's Bay.

It was the beginning of July when we left Stromness in the

Orkney Islands and the 14th of August when we reached York Factory. Our ship, the *Prince of Wales*, cast anchor at a place called Five-Fathom Hole on Hayes River, where ships could swing safely at anchor. As soon as she was sighted from the lookout at York Factory, a packet manned by six oars came to meet us, collect the letters, and take Captain J. D. Herd ashore.

Also a sloop of about twelve tons came to take off the passengers and as much cargo as she could carry. It was the season for storms and a terrific one now was raging. The voyage from England to York Factory seemed always to be attended by storms, Captain Herd said, while good weather and fair winds enabled the ship to make the return trips in something like twenty-one days.

We got aboard the sloop, which was an open boat with two masts, and headed for shore. We had no provisions. The storm buffeted us unmercifully and it took our marvellous native Indian boatmen, who knew every shoal and sandbar in the region, a day and a half to make the six miles. We arrived at the Factory wet, cold, and hungry.

The yearly arrival of the English ship at York Factory was a great event and caused much excitement. It had to be unloaded, loaded again, and off before the season advanced. Apart from unloading the merchandise which the ship brought, the cargoes of furs brought by the brigades from the various inland posts of the Company had to be checked and the accounts of the officers who accompanied them carefully examined and made ready for London. Night shifts were provided and work went on day and night.

The *Prince of Wales* stood at anchor in Five-Fathom Hole for a week, exchanging cargoes. Sloops took packages of furs to the ship and returned with the much-needed goods brought from England. The merchandise was hoisted from the sloops to the pier by a donkey engine.

Beached on the shores at York Factory were the boats of the brigades that had come from the interior—the Saskatchewan, Edmonton, Carlton, and Cumberland brigades—all loaded with furs. There were three boats to a brigade and eight men to a boat. The boatmen had set up their tents in orderly fashion, using oars for tent poles and moose or buffalo hides, or boat tarpaulins, for coverings. Before each tent a small fire glowed.

It was a great sight for my English eyes and, even yet, the memory of that scene at York Factory long ago has power to move me. An English trading post, colourful voyageurs, Indians of many tribes speaking different languages and dancing and singing in happy companionship, red fires against a black night; the *Prince of Wales* standing at sea, taking on the wealth of the great North.

The brigades assembled here had all come down the Saskatchewan River to the Grand Rapid, across Lake Winnipeg to Norway House, and on to York Factory. The round trip from Edmonton to York Factory and back took three months; from Carlton, two and a half months; Cumberland, two months; Saskatchewan, two months. Their cargoes consisted mostly of buffalo robes and pemmican. The pemmican was for the York Factory post.

On the night of the ship's arrival, the Company gave a regale of rum (half a tumbler) to each man. This regale was weak stuff—a pint of rum to a gallon of water. As boxing was one of the chief entertainments for the voyageurs upon their arrival at a post, half an hour after the regale was issued, a boxing match was arranged. There were some noted boxers in the brigades and each brigade had its prize boxer. He was called the bully or *chanté-la-coque*.

Now with studied unconcern and a dash of gallantry, the champion boxer of the post challenged the bully from another brigade. Well, on my first night at York Factory, I saw the cleverest and most skilful boxing that I have ever witnessed. Each winner fought in turn the bully from other brigades until the championship was decided. It was a great victory to be pronounced the bully of York Factory as this was the seaport of the Company and had a large territory tributary to it.

I was a curious fellow and when I saw how hard the voyageurs worked, I enquired about their payment. I discovered that the wages of an ordinary boatman (middleman) was two made beaver a day. This was equal to one dollar; the bowman got two and a half made beaver a day; a steersman got three. The guide received the same wages as the oarsman, with a bonus of five pounds, or twenty dollars, at the end of the trip. A made beaver at York Factory up to 1871 represented thirty-five cents. The farther one went inland, the higher the value of the beaver became. This was due to the extra expense of travelling. At Cumberland House the value of a made beaver was fifty cents; at Mackenzie River seventy-five cents. These values would entirely depend on the time and the place. Made beaver values were always fluctuating.

MADE BEAVER	
FUR	MADE BEAVER OR SKINS (TOKENS)
Beaver	12
Bear	20
Ermine	$^1/_2$
Fisher	30
Fox (Red)	10
Fox (Silver)	150
Lynx	10
Marten	10
Mink	5
Musquash	$^1/_4$
Otter	25

The rations of the men consisted of two pounds of pemmican and a pound of flour a day. Two pounds of sugar, a pound of tea, and a pound of tobacco (eighteen plugs to the pound) was the weekly allowance for the boat crew. The tobacco was imported from the West Indies.

My introduction to James R. Clare, the chief factor at York Factory, was rather informal. On my first day at the post, I jumped up on the big platform that led from the wharf to the storage depot, not knowing that only officers in charge of the "stuff" of the post and the incoming cargo were allowed on it.

An old fellow dressed in a fine blue cloth capote (cloak and hood) decorated with large brass buttons came towards me. I took him for some sort of boss. "Young man," he said, "get off this platform before I kick you off." Well, I had a bit of pride and besides, I was a graduate officer of Sandhurst Military Academy and accustomed to being spoken to respectfully. "You are pretty rude, my man," I said.

The old fellow made a lunge for me. Well, I was young, supple, and skilled in boxing. I hit out at the fellow and started in to give him a good trouncing. He was a good fighter, too. I was getting the best of the match when a couple of men ran up from the dock and separated us. "Fool!" said one. "What do you mean by fighting the chief factor?" I am glad to admit that I did not apologize.

That evening the second officer of the post informed me that the factor was returning me to England for insubordination. I packed up my things without regret. Next morning when Captain Herd came ashore, the factor informed him of my dismissal from the service. This did not suit Captain Herd at all. My people were pretty influential in the Company. He insisted on hearing my side of the story.

"I don't see any insubordination in the thing," he told the factor. "Ensign King did not know about the autocratic regulations that prevail here. You began the attack, King defended himself. I refuse to take him back to England without an order from the London Board. You will have to refer the matter to the governors at Fort Garry." Clare decided to send me to Fort Garry with the Red River brigade.

Clare was a clever man and a good accountant. He was the son of a piano manufacturer in England. Only one of the five clerks who came out from England with me was kept at York Factory. As a rule, apprentice clerks were given the particular kind of work for which they were fitted and placed where most needed. That evening Mrs. Clare sent for me. She was the daughter of the Thomas Sinclair who helped Donald Gunn write his *History of Manitoba*. Gunn came out as a crofter, but rose to become justice of the peace in the Red River Settlement. Mrs. Clare asked me to apologize to her husband, but I refused. I do not think she had much patience with her husband's disagreeable autocratic ways.

I was amused to discover that the meals at York Factory were presided over with the discipline and ceremony of an officers' barracks. Chief Factor Clare sat at the head of the table, his second officer at the foot, and, on the right of the second officer, the chief guide. Next to the chief factor, on each side, sat the chief factors who had come down with the brigades. Clerks of all grades filled up the remainder of the space. The post missionary was generally a guest. A decanter of port wine stood at one end of the table. There wasn't much liquor served—about a tumblerful all around. Everything was conducted in strict military fashion. The bell that hung in the belfry of the fort announced meals, work—all routine duties.

When I was leaving York Factory, Mrs. Clare gave me a bottle of the factor's best wine, a cake, and a letter of introduction to Mrs. Graham, the wife of the chief factor at Norway House.

Mrs. Graham welcomed me with the utmost kindness and gave me a letter to the wife of Governor Dallas at Fort Garry. Governor Dallas was, at this time, the head of the Company in Canada. Mrs. Dallas was the daughter of Governor Douglas of the Vancouver post. Instead of getting me into trouble, this clash with Clare seemed to increase my popularity with the ladies. I was received with great kindness by Governor and Mrs. Dallas at Fort Garry.

There is a reason for everything, however. Governor Dallas knew my father's elder brother, Sir Richard King, in England, and as the governor did not know I was in the country until I arrived at Fort Garry, I became a sort of protégé of his. In the autumn of 1862, Governor Dallas appointed me assistant clerk to Chief Trader Alexander Murray, who was in charge of the lower fort.

CHAPTER 2

I Go on a Trading Trip

Trading parties were going out and I was anxious to join one. George Davis, manager of the Fort Garry fur-trading shop, said, "I'll send you on a trading trip with four picked men and two dog teams; four dogs and two men to each team. You will visit the territory along Lake Winnipeg from Fort Garry as far as Berens River on the east side of the lake and across to Grindstone Point on the west." The year was 1862–63. I was a greenhorn.

We selected our cargo and packed it on the sleds: four hundred pounds of trade goods to each sled, and one hundred pounds each of dog feed, ammunition, and provisions, which we called our private dunnage. Powder, shot, and flints were the most important items. Flints were little pieces of stone about an inch square which we imported from England. We used flintlock guns. Ten flints bought a beaver skin.

I was interested in the large supply of muskrat spears we had to take. These were two-and-a-half-inch spears attached to nine-inch rods of iron made by Company blacksmiths from rod iron brought from England. We lashed these spears on top of the loads. Other trading goods were cheap calico and prints, both broad and narrow, which sold for twenty-five cents a yard. By cheap, I mean cheap for the time and in a new country. Company goods were not shoddy goods. They were the best obtainable. We took bolts of flannel. In present-day currency, the selling price of this was twenty-five cents a yard. Our invoice included fancy, showy-coloured rugs and blankets for summer trade and heavy Hudson's Bay point blankets for winter trade; great quantities of coloured beads, fine beads for embroidery (twenty-five cents a skein) and large for the necklaces which the Indians favoured; ribbons of all widths and coloured silks; thread, needles, and thimbles of brass and silver; knives, axes, files, pots, and pans made at York Factory by our own tinsmiths from sheet tin brought from England; shirts, fine and common; good rolled Virginia tobacco which we imported and which came twisted like a rope, and for which we got one dollar a pound; a few pairs of moleskin or fustian trousers; plain Indian rubbers and overshoes, which we traded for two skins valued at one dollar; woollen socks; tea, valued at one dollar a pound; sugar, fifty cents the pound; a few pounds of biscuits; and lard at fifty cents for the pound.

At that time, in the interior of the country, food, except meat, was a luxury. Anything to eat, no matter what, sold at the rate of one dollar a pound. We packed a good supply of two-ounce bags of vermilion, which the men said would go like hot cakes at seventy-five cents a bag. Mostly, the Indians used native paints, which they prepared themselves, but they found the Company paint beautifying and of deeper colour than their own and were prepared to pay for it.

We packed, too, a good supply of little, round looking glasses. These were always in great demand, the men said, and one of the best articles of trade. The Indians carried these little mirrors constantly on their hunting and scouting expeditions and could decoy game—ducks, buffalo, deer—right up to them. They were perfect for signalling. The Indians, I was told, were master heliographers and were able to flash messages of danger—the approach of buffalo herds or the appearance of strangers—from hill to hill and so to distant tribes.

I had proof of the heliographic skill of the Indians a good many years later when I was stationed, in 1900, at York Factory. One day when Reverend Mr. Faries was in my office, the Métis chief from Split Lake arrived. "What is the news?" I asked him. He answered, "*Hugamoeskaoo*. (Oh! Not much). The big Master's wife is dead." We did not know whether he meant the Queen of England or Mrs. Chipman, the commissioner's wife. Three months later when the ship arrived from England, we learned that Queen Victoria was dead.

By checking dates with Commissioner Chipman when he came to the Factory some months later, we discovered that two days after news of Queen Victoria's death had reached Fort Garry the Split Lake chief knew it. He must have got it by heliograph from eastern Canada and had come to tell me and get a cup of tea and a little present.

The men Davis assigned to this trip were the most reliable runners and traders at the Fort Garry post—George Kipling, senior; Thomas Lyons; Joe Monkman; and Daniel Thomas. Officially, I was boss of this outfit. In effect, I was only clerk to Kipling, who was an experienced hunter, trader, and a man of high standing in the service of the Company. While rated a most reliable servant, traveller, and Indian trader, he was chiefly noted as the famous packet carrier from Fort Garry to Norway House. He was a native of St. Peter's band, born more or less in the service of the Company, of Orkney or Shetland and Indian extraction.

Kipling's scheduled time for the round trip from Fort Garry to Norway House and back, a distance of approximately three hundred miles, was from December 1 to December 20. He walked thirty-five miles a day, more or less, depending on the weather. He was never known to lose the mail or to be behind his schedule.

He travelled on snowshoes, either carrying the packet or hauling it on a four-foot sled. In addition to the Hudson's Bay packet—letters and documents with an average weight of twenty to twenty-five pounds—he carried ten to twelve pounds of provisions, enough to last him from post to post, and bedding and clothes to the weight of fifteen pounds. Always he travelled alone. He carried no firearms.

His equipment was a nicely cut four-foot pole with a piece of chisel-shaped steel attached to one end, a medium-sized hunting knife, a one-and-a-half-pound chopping axe, a covered copper kettle (the first size), and a tin cup. The cup and kettle went into a small bag which he hung in front of his toboggan. His daily ration was figured by Company method: one and a half pounds pemmican, one pound of fat bacon, half a pound of bannock, a little tea, sugar, tobacco, sulphur, and made matches. The total weight of his load at starting was about fifty pounds, growing lighter each day as his rations decreased.

No matter how cold the weather, he wore ordinary clothes: moccasins, wool socks, light fawn skin capote, rug, and leggings of the same light skin. These were the lightest and warmest travelling clothes available. He slept in his blankets, sled upturned against the weather. Kipling had an adopted son, named for him, who in later years became a trusted packet carrier in the Athabasca District and the far North.

Joe Monkman was a man of forty, four feet ten in height, and weighed one hundred and sixty pounds. He, too, was a reliable temporary servant of the Company, known as a small Company trader. Foolish Joe he was called, because he was mischievous. He was no fool, however, but a most reliable hunter and trader. He could speak English, French, and Plains Cree and Saulteaux. The Company gave him a bonus for the furs he brought and on the goods he sold. A sharp trader, he disregarded the rules laid down for tariffs and business generally, acting on his own judgment, and never failed to show a profit for himself and for the Company.

Joe's methods were original. Upon reaching an Indian encampment, before trading, he gave each man and woman a drink of rum. When he left, an Indian woman generally disappeared with him. He discarded her before reaching the next camp, where he took another. The Indians regarded this conduct as one of Joe's customs and harboured no ill will against him.

Joe once took a visiting nobleman in his cariole by dog team (six dogs) from Fort Garry to Montreal, where he drove his lordship about the streets of the city in great style. To his delight, the bright *tapis* (dog clothes) with flying ribbons and bells ringing terrified the horses and tied up the traffic. On his return trip, Joe brought a paying passenger. This man never reached Fort Garry. No inquiry was made, but for a long time thereafter Joe had considerable cheap jewellery for trading purposes.

Daniel Thomas and Thomas Lyons were also celebrated dog train drivers and runners.

Like Kipling, Daniel Thomas was a famous packet carrier of the North. At eighteen, he made his first trip with the boat brigade to York Factory. In time he rose to be boss of the brigade. He carried the packet between Lac Du Brochet and Cumberland House. As a post runner, he traded in Eskimo territory, gathering great quantities of Arctic fox skins.

Daniel left the Company in 1895 and came out to civilization, but every winter until he was past eighty, he returned to his old trapping grounds at Lac Du Brochet. He called himself the Boss of Traverse Bay.

We had some wonderful men among what outsiders called half-breeds in those days, men of mixed blood. In the Company, we called them the *bois-brûlés* (burnt wood or brown colour) or Métis. We regarded these men highly and never forgot they were important to the fur trade. They *were* the fur trade.

It was the middle of March when we left Fort Garry, walking and running behind our toboggans. At a command from Kipling, the dogs bounded forward. All around us was a dark, grey world. Dawn had not yet broken. We wore light clothing and light wool stockings and light moccasins. We would have to walk every foot of our way.

After some delay, we were skirting the east side of Lake Winnipeg as Davis had instructed. We came upon a chance Indian camp and got their furs. We visited Fort Alexander to get provisions and a list of Indians indebted to this post in the hope of collecting from them, but did not trade in this territory, as Fort Alexander was an established post.

On we travelled, Thomas Lyons leading. He was never known to lose his way. He was a peculiar looking man—a Scotch Métis from St. Peter's Reserve. He, too, was a temporary employee from Lower Fort Garry. Five feet in height, he walked with a slouching gait, a gliding step. With his big head, red, watery eyes, short body, and long legs and arms, he looked like an animated walking machine. He walked at the rate of five miles an hour, weather regulating his speed. Always he had a compass strapped to his wrist, though the stars, moon, sun, and native instincts were his chief guides. He was liked and respected by us all. Of the Scottish type, he was capital company, though inclined to be sullen at times. He was intelligent and he could be nice when it suited him. Like all native bois-brûlés, he was a good fiddler, playing by ear—with variations.

Like Monkman, he was unique in his methods of trading and always came out on top. An Indian linguist, he could sing, dance, and—gamble. His sleight of hand generally ended in his skinning the Indians out of their entire fur catch. They forgave him, however, as he was a nice fellow and had given them well-watered rum.

On one of his trading trips for me, he ran into the runners for Bannatyne, McDermott, and an American trader, who had arrived at the camps ahead of him and collected all the furs. Lyons proposed a feast and dance to drink up all the rum. He said he had a supply of Company trading goods and the Company could well stand a treat. When the party was well underway, Tom's chance came—gambling. Towards morning, he packed up his furs—having cleaned the American out—and left, taking along an Indian woman. He got every fur, not as a result of trading but gambling. When he reached me at Berens River, I was somewhat surprised and anxious over the results, but it passed off all right.

We kept on skirting the shore of the lake, but did not come across any more Indian camps. Kipling felt bothered. Presently, we fell in with a hunter who told us that the bands had gone to the big medicine feast at Blood Vein River about twenty-five or thirty miles southeast of Berens River. This, Kipling said, would be a gathering of crack medicine men from all over the country. We hurried on.

Back from the river in a fine open space, surrounded by timber, we found the great medicine tent set up. Around it at respectable distances stood the tents of the different tribes. To this great ceremony had come all the principal medicine men from as far as Lake Superior and from the north and west.

The inner, or medicine, tent was enclosed by a great outer tent one hundred feet in circumference covered with the leather lodge coverings borrowed from the assembled tribes, who were themselves living in birch bark teepees which they had temporarily erected.

The framework of the outer lodge consisted of a fence of stout posts which, ten feet apart, were driven two or three feet into the ground and extended seven or eight above. In the inner circle four men and a woman (their most sincere and expert doctors) were conjuring. In the large circular corridor between the outer and inner circles, the lesser medicine men, headmen, men of standing, and drummers chanted, played tom-toms, and cried weird songs. The general crowd was kept outside the medicine tent.

It was a spectacle: a dark night—weird, excited, terrifying music and yelling issued from the great tent. Tiny streams of smoke rose from the open fires before the teepees. We were a few white men among more than a hundred (not including their families) frenzied, almost naked Indians.

At first I looked on with amusement, then with interest when I saw that the conjurors in the inner tent—with their drum-beating, exhortations, screaming, and dancing—actually made the tent and the stout outer posts of the walls tremble. Noted ventriloquists, these doctors filled the air with the cries of animals and birds.

Kipling and I were outside the great tent. I urged him to use his influence with the Indians to let me in. They refused to listen to him, but I gave the principal man a present and after several clever moves, he got me into the outer circle. Here I did my best with one of the lesser chiefs. I would get nowhere as I was, he told me, so he vermilioned my face and hands, gave me his head-gear, calumet, and blanket, and said he would try to pass me off as a visiting medicine man and so get me into the inner circle. He warned me not to speak but only to chant some meaningless Indian words which he chanted for me.

By the magic word, *skitewar*, he got the attention of a doctor in the inner tent, who poked his head through the foot of the tent under the skin wall. Suddenly a bag was thrown over my head, and somehow or other—and to this day I cannot say how it was managed—I was swiftly hauled into the inner tent and my head uncovered.

A woman grabbed me by the shoulders, threw off my blanket, tore my shirt sleeves apart, and, before I knew what she was about, slashed my arm in two places with a sharp flint. Blood spurted from the gashes. She put her mouth to the wound and sucked my blood. Now she commanded me to slash her arm and suck her blood. I was thoroughly alarmed. But these conjurors were in such a frenzy that I dared not disobey. I slashed her arm and sucked her blood.

By this ceremony, I was to learn later, I had become a medicine man. They had admitted me to their craft. At once my fellow conjurors began to show me their medicines. They had little bundles of medicine of every description, all neatly tied in separate packages. They had *powogans* (evil spirits) cut out of bark, roots, and metal, and charms of every description. Some medicine was for cures; some for poisoning their enemies. Each bundle was different. These Indian doctors practised a lot of humbug to fool the tribes, such as throwing their voices in the air and imitating the voices of evil spirits to threaten their audiences. Yet, as a member of their guild, I must confess that, in my long years among the tribes, I have seen these medicine men make some marvellous cures.

No amount of money would have admitted me to this inner circle. Now, since I was one of them, they wouldn't let me out. The upshot of my adoption into this Indian medical brotherhood was that, by trading in the vicinity of the medicine tent, we succeeded in getting every fur that the red men possessed.

We had a great demand for our rat spears and on this trip I learned how muskrats were speared. One day, upon reaching a regular camping place of an important band of Indians and finding it empty, Kipling said, "They must be after rats. We'll track them." We located the band on the lake spearing muskrats. I found this an interesting business. As soon as they saw us, every man, woman, and child wanted to buy spears.

Muskrats have two houses: those which they build on top of the ice for sunning themselves during the winter months[2] and their permanent houses built on the banks of rivers and lakes partly above, and partly under, water. From these permanent houses they have little runs to their sunrooms on top of the ice. These runs remain open, even in the severest weather, due to the constant movement of water as the animals swim back and forth. If ice forms, it is so thin that the muskrats can be seen and speared as they journey back and forth.

The entrance or tunnel into a muskrat sunroom is under water, up through the bottom and centre of the house. It is the south sides of the permanent muskrat houses that Indian hunters generally attack, which, due to sun exposure, are thinner than the others.

The hunter drives his spear through the muskrat house and when he feels a rat wriggling on the end of it, he detaches the handle, which is from six to eight feet long, leaving the spear in the rat. Then he pokes his hand up through the bottom of the house, cautiously, to avoid the rat's dangerous teeth, and draws the spear and his furry victim out. To prevent bruising the pelt, thereby decreasing its market value, he kills the rat by giving it a crack on the head.

A muskrat family consists of from six to eight in the first (May) litter; eight or ten in the second (middle of June) litter; and from ten to fourteen in the third (August) litter. The first-born batch has a litter of young in the fall; the other litters do not produce young that fall. The largest number of full-grown muskrats I have known to pass a winter in a muskrat house was twenty.

I have often seen muskrat houses broken open to disclose only skeletons of a colony of rats. Minks, having discovered these rat runs, had crawled into the permanent homes and caught the rats as they returned from their sunbaths. A mink will stay concealed in one of these muskrat houses until he has caught the whole colony.

For small muskrat pelts, we paid at the rate of a shilling for five; for medium skins, a shilling for three; for a real fine spring muskrat, we paid sixpence. The Company sold these pelts in England for two shillings each. Rival traders complained that we made a double profit, one on the pelts, one on the trading goods. They did not figure that the Company had a big overhead expense.

I was sorry when our trip ended. We had travelled through hard weather, sleeping on frozen ground or on beds of spruce boughs. This trip, however, gave me an insight into the trading business. We estimated the value of our trading trip at one thousand dollars. George Davis, head of the fur shop, was good enough to say I was the first young clerk of the Company who had conducted a successful trip in this region. The credit was due Kipling and my other experienced and reliable men.

Back at Fort Garry, I was given a funny kind of job. I had to shoot pigeons for the officers' mess. My payment was a shilling a bushel. Pigeons were so thick in the country at this time that they darkened the skies in passing. The old post records contain numerous references to these migratory pigeons that were smaller than tame pigeons. Manitoba was a feeding ground for the flocks, especially the region around Lower Fort Garry.

Naline hazelnuts (we called them monkey nuts) grew abundantly in the country too and they, like the pigeons, were a source of revenue for the settlers. The payment for the nuts was the same as for pigeons, a shilling the bushel.

As part of my training, the head clerk gave me the minutes of council to copy. Though the copying was boring, I found these minutes, which went as far back as 1821, to the time of the joining of the Hudson's Bay Company with The Nor'Westers, highly interesting. The company required the writing in their post journals to be not only legible but uniform; therefore, it was part of each apprentice's training to practise the Company's style of penmanship.

Another practice piece that the clerk gave me was a petition for a detachment of soldiers which the Company had drawn up for submission to the London office, instructing me to make copies and to post them at the places of importance in the colony: Lower Fort Garry, St. Andrew's Church, Upper Fort Garry, the Settlement of Headingly, St. Peters, and the Indian settlement.

The end of this petition read: "And your petitioners as in duty bound will ever pray ..." I was seventeen and liked a prank. This copybook stuff was dull so to liven it a bit, I substituted the word "prey" for "pray." Up went my revised copies. They provided fun for the people in the colony, but Judge Black was not entirely pleasant about my practical joke. Neither was Chief Trader Alexander Murray.

Whether it was because of my liking for jokes or not, I cannot say, but at any rate I was detailed to the job of collecting accounts. This work took me, on horseback, from St. Peters to Headingly. In a short time, I got to know every man, woman, and child in the settlement, and I soon became a sort of authority on the various relationships existing among these Red River settlers.

The Red River people were a kindly lot and very hospitable. There were no newspapers in those days, and travellers who brought news were heartily welcomed. When one was sighted, a man or woman would stand on the trail in front of his or her house and, with cap or apron, wave him in.

The Red River houses were built of fine logs that had been rafted down the Red River. These logs were squared on one side, as smooth as if planed. The Red River axemen were artists.

Visitors to the Red River homes were given a place at the body of the long, scoured deal table, which was always open to governor or officer, trader, Métis, or whoever chanced to pass. From his place at the head of the table, with his family around him, the Red River host was his own man, proud and genial. He recognized no social distinction, but gave hospitality to all. It was a good age, I told myself, as I went about the settlement. It was akin to Chaucer's age.

At eight o'clock every morning, I started out. Outside of my regular pay, I was allowed seventy-five cents a day for provisions, but as the settlers would not take payment for my meals, I returned the three shillings to the office at the end of each day. I rendered an account of my collections every Saturday before noon.

There was no money in the country and business was conducted by the simple system of barter. The settlers all ran accounts with the Company. On presenting the Company's bills and asking the debtors how they proposed to pay, they offered whatever they had to give—a cow or calf, a pony, so many days' work, a month at woodcutting or haymaking, or a trip in the boats.

I must confess that I was a poor judge of the livestock they offered, but I did the best I could. As a rule I came out pretty well. The barter system was a sort of "no pay no credit" business and it worked very well. There were no lawyers in the settlement, the nearest approach to one being Thomas Gunn.

The Red River people were good dancers and some of the clerks enjoyed going to the local Red River jig parties. I went to one, and I must say that I did not enjoy the fighting that went on amongst the women when their men were monopolized. This form of entertainment was strange to me. I got ragged by the other clerks for being a "stuck-up blue blood."

After the dances, however, the women appeared to forget their quarrels. On the whole, they were a neighbourly lot, lending anything they possessed, from food to cradles, to one another. A woman going to make a cup of tea might have to run around to several cabins before she found her teakettle.

I find it hard to imagine the great city of Winnipeg overlying the Fort Garry of long ago. The first fire engine used in the Red River Settlement was a very simple affair. Pierre Jarand was the official fireman and he had to drive his ox cart a quarter of a mile to the river to pump (ship's pump) a barrel of water. Pierre always clung to his pipe and went on smoking no matter how serious the fire.

The Company post office at Fort Garry was run by a Mrs. Bannatyne and her son, in connection with her small grocery store, which was on the site of the present Alexandria Hotel. Mrs. Bannatyne's pay was a pound a month. Every evening she sent the mail to the Company's general post office. It used to amuse me to see this post mistress pay a customer a shilling for produce, then receive the shilling back for the postage of a letter.

CHAPTER 3

I Leave for Mackenzie's River

It was my fight with the bully of the Athabaska brigade that sent me to Mackenzie's river. One day a long train of freighters arrived from Edmonton with a cargo of pemmican and robes. I was sitting on a counter in the trading shop with my back to the body of it, helping myself to gingersnaps out of a keg that had just been opened, when I heard someone call, "Boy! Boy!" I took no notice. I was only visiting in the shop.

All at once a heavy hand caught me by the neck and bent me backward over the counter. I couldn't break my assailant's grip, so I grabbed the hammer on the counter that had been used to open the keg of gingersnaps and gave the fellow a crack. His grip loosened and he fell sprawling on the floor, unconscious.

"He is dead! Arrest that clerk!" cried a number of the freighters who were in the shop trading.

Well, I was interned in the fort to wait for the fellow to live or die. Eight weeks later, when he came to, I was hauled before chief factors Dallas and McTavish. "So you're killing our men! First you fight the governor of York Factory, now you knock out Paulet Paul, the champion bully of the Athabaska brigade. You are not making a very good beginning in the Company, you hot-headed young aristocrat!" they accused.

"In both instances, sirs," I said, "I was unfairly attacked. I make no apologies. Even my father, who is a British officer, would have said, 'Well done, my boy! Death before dishonour!'"

"You are too spirited for the colony. We'll send you to Mackenzie's river to cool your hot British blood a bit!" said Mr. Dallas.

One day, a goodly time later, the chief factor sent for me. "It is the first of June," said he. "The Red River brigade leaves on the third. We have decided to send you north with it." I was a bit taken back, I must confess, but I answered, "You meant what you said about sending me to Mackenzie's river? Well, I am looking forward to the adventure."

"You'll find hard work and responsibility there," he answered. "Many of the young clerks in the North complain about the dullness." "The fur business is never dull!" I said. The chief factor smiled. "The North is one place where men of imagination are needed. You'll do well in the northern service," he said.

That was a great day, the day we left the fort. On the banks of the Red River lay the first section of the brigade—three boats— ready to set off on their long journey. Through the banging of guns, the salute of cannon, the cheering of the crowds, I was aware of a great uplift. The whole colony, about three or four hundred people, had come to cheer us on our way.

Baptiste Bruce, the well-known boat guide of the North, was in charge. Under his sharp, quick commands, the crew looked to their cargo. Bruce inspected it himself, examining the lashings carefully. The complement of each boat was seventy-five to one hundred packages of one hundred pounds each and the value estimated at five thousand dollars. The cargo load of the entire brigade, nine boats, was estimated at forty-five thousand to fifty thousand dollars.

All this cargo was entrusted to one man, Baptiste Bruce, for safe carriage over the treacherous waters to Methye Portage. I can still hear Bruce's commands. They came short and clear. At his word, when everything about the long, low, open boats had been made safe, the crew fell into their places. We had a crew of eight men: a steersman, a bowman, and six middlemen. Although I was the officer in charge of the brigade, I took the place Bruce gave me with the men.

Suddenly, through the noise of the send-off, one word rang

out: *embarque!* That call was more potent than any military reveille. With a shout the men grasped their oars. The boats shot out from their moorings. The men sang in time to their oars. In the bow of my boat Baptiste Bruce stood like a figurehead, calm, rigid. As we drew farther and farther away, the voices of the crowd, whose very existence depended upon the returns of the fur cargoes, grew fainter. I looked at the rowers. Beads of sweat stood round and silvery on their hairy breasts and between their powerful brown shoulders. The great voyage had begun!

Away we went! A slight wind filled the sails and carried the boat down the river, relieving the oarsmen. Only the bowman and steersman stood in their places. I sat atop the cargo, thrilled. "Too bad," I said after awhile, "that the second section of the brigade isn't with us. In case of trouble, they could stand by."

"Nothing like that!" said Bruce. "We have men enough here to handle anything. You will see! Suppose we and Alexis L'Esperance, with the second section of this brigade, should arrive at the rapids and the portages together? There is not enough room on the portages. The men would be standing on one foot while we unloaded, portaged our cargo, and hauled our boats up the river. There is plenty of reason why L'Esperance should not leave the fort for two or three days yet!"

Well, being a greenhorn, I didn't see, but I let it go. After awhile the wind died down. Even when the wind was right we could make only fair speed, drifting. I began to think it was a pretty tame business. I moved about, examining the boat furnishings and chatting with the men who sat or lay upon the taut tarpaulins. The sun was hot.

I was the clerk in charge of this great brigade bound for Fort Simpson, thence back to York Factory. I was responsible for supervising the landing and receiving of cargoes at the portages and posts. I had the responsibility of the delivery and reception of official letters at each post on our route. I should have felt a man of affairs. I knew that I was not much more than supercargo. I felt mighty green.

The actual commander of the brigade was Baptiste Bruce. From the moment he put his foot into the first boat of the brigade until the boat touched shore, no matter where, he was in complete command. No other officer of the Company, no matter what his rank—even the governor of the Company himself—dared interfere. There was wisdom in these rules as you will see.

Great fellows, those guides, and so were the boatmen. Their physique would do credit to the ancient Greeks. How they could sing! In Gaelic, French, English, and Indian of many dialects.

The York boats appeared in the fur trade between 1746 and 1795. In outline a York boat was just like the old Orkney boat. With a figurehead added, shields lashed to the sides, and a coloured square sail it might easily be taken for a Viking ship of old. These boats were built in the colony by Company ship-builders and were designed to travel over lakes, rapids, and rivers.

York boats were carefully and solidly built and had great beauty of line. The builders spent days in the bush selecting the right spruce from which the bow and stern pieces could be cut. These boats were sometimes called Great North canoes, although they had no relation to North canoes which were made of birch bark and were twenty-five to thirty feet long.

These York boats were built in two sizes, one from twenty-eight to thirty-three feet long, and an eight-foot beam, and a larger one of forty feet.

Quite recently the last of the York boats was discovered at Norway House where she lay after having spent her last years as a barge used for the towing of hay. In the winter of 1934–35 she was made seaworthy and fitted out with sweeps. In the summer she made her last portage. She was towed down Lake Winnipeg from Norway House to Selkirk and from there trucked to Lower Fort Garry. This once-proud freighter has become a museum piece. It is forty feet long, ten feet wide, with bow and stern posts cut in at an angle of forty-five degrees, which enabled her to be shoved off any obstructions she might meet in the rapids. She could carry 110 pieces of 90 pounds each with a crew of a steersman, eight middlemen, and a bowman.

I began to look about and examine our outfit. We had no luxuries. Three pounds was the gross weight of food allowed each man on the bill of lading. It consisted of a little pemmican, tea, a bit of flour, and some tobacco. For dunnage, the middlemen were allowed fifteen pounds, the steersman twenty pounds. This food was supplied on the outgoing trip at Fort Garry, Norway House, Cumberland House, and Portage La Loche and on the return trip at the same places. Two very important articles were a tool chest and a medicine chest. The medicine chest, equipped according to the formula of the Company's doctor in London, contained:

> 2 pounds of epsom salts (crystals)
> 1 dozen purgative powders
> 1 dozen vomits (in little packets)
> 1 small spirits smelling salts
> ½ dozen bottles painkiller (medium size)
> 1 or 2 rolls of sticking plaster
> A lancet
> A pair of forceps

There was a book of instructions with these drugs, but none of the men, not even the guide, could read them. However, they knew the doses of everything by heart. A guide never gave a man medicine to administer to himself. He was required to fetch his pannikin—a tin dish that held a pint—filled with river water and the guide poured out what he thought to be a dose. This the patient had to drink under his observation. This was to prevent men from shamming sickness. There was very little deception practised, however. When it came to extracting a tooth, the guide set his patient up against the side of the boat, got a firm grip of the tooth with forceps, and hauled it out. A jackknife was all that was required for an amputation. Everything was managed very well.

I looked at the tool chest box, which a boatman said might mean life or death to us. He was so earnest that I examined the contents carefully. There was a hammer, axe, handsaw, a bundle of assorted cut nails, brace-and-bit, gimlet, three assorted chisels, caulking irons, oakum, a pail of tar, a couple of yards of spare canvas, assorted thread (this was lift thread that came in little bundles and was sold by the pound), two sail needles, a half-dozen awls, and some *babiche* (rawhide cut into thin strips for mending clothes and sails).

As I stood in the hot sun that morning of long ago and realized that every item we had aboard had been planned with attention to economy of space and weight and use, I felt impressed.

I remember asking a boatman about the equipment of the boat itself. This included a large axe, three eight-gallon tin boat kettles, a two-quart bailing pan, extra sail and rigging, a pair of spare oars, a removable steering rudder, and a bundle of straps.

I asked Baptiste Bruce about the carrying straps. He said, "There are ten to the bundle. We use them on the portages. Each man is given one, and I, or another guide, put the names of the men on them. We are very careful of those straps and, at the end of the trip, these straps must be returned to me. Suppose a man loses his strap? Then he must buy another. And, how he will grumble if he has to buy a second strap out of his hard-earned money! When a man pays for a thing, he is careful. Is that not right, Noel?"

Noel, who was tuning up his fiddle, answered, "You are right, Baptiste. It is hard-earned money for sure! But the life of a boatman—it is one big, full life. Me? I would rather be in this Red River brigade than—than anything else. It is one big honour for a man to be picked for a boatman for Bruce's brigade."

"Hurrah for Bruce!" He jumped to his feet, waved his fiddle, and stepped out a vigorous jig while the men kept time with their hands.

Bruce walked away, and Noel spoke again. He said, "The money is not everything on a trip like this. It is the honour of being picked for this service. Sixteen pounds for the round trip is the pay of an ordinary boatman. But the steersman gets twenty pounds, because he has the responsibility! The foreman has a hard job too, and he gets eighteen pounds. Bruce gets twenty-five pounds, and, if results are good, a bonus at the end of the trip. He has many privileges too, like being allowed to mess with the officer in charge of the brigade, generally the chief factor. This time it is yourself, the clerk. But me? I am lucky on this trip. Baptiste Bruce has picked me for your camp attendant to cook for you. For this I get two pounds extra. And I will get better food."

I felt surprised and pleased to hear that I had been given a personal servant. Noel was repacking his dunnage bag. I noticed that he had one three-point Hudson's Bay blanket, a pair of ten-ounce duck trousers and a duck frock—this was a kind of shirt that hung loose over the trousers—a small towel, a cake of soap, a comb, a looking glass, and a couple of pairs of moccasins. These fellows certainly could travel light. Yet, what more did a man need?

We started at noon from Lower Fort Garry and drifted down the river—about twenty miles. During the night a strong, fair wind rose, which filled our sails and carried us along.

At 3:00 AM, when we got out on Lake Winnipeg, the wind arose to a storm. To my surprise, Bruce headed out into the middle of the lake.

"*Towich!*" commanded Bruce. The crew came alive. The vigour of that command brought me to attention, too. The men, dragging their starboard oars, swerved the boat and with long strokes steered straight out to open water.

"What does 'towich' mean?" I asked. But though I stood immediately above the oarsman, my voice came faint through the hoarse wind. "'Out into the open lake.' It is Cree," he answered. Then he roared a curse of defiance as an avalanche of water raked the boat from stem to stern. Without missing a stroke, the men got out of their wet jackets and, bare-bodied, doubled to their oars.

A long hour passed. The wind rose to a gale. Bruce moved to the steersman. Through the roar of wind and water, his orders came distinct. "The other boats," he commanded, "must not be allowed to catch up to us or come nearer than two hundred yards. They must not pass us!" He watched to see that when he hoisted or slackened sail, the men in the other boats did likewise.

Now Bruce took the steersman's place. The wind had grown dangerous. Bruce's voice, iron-cool, reached every man. Still his orders were distinct and unhurried. He said: "Put the smoked moose tarpaulins (covering from fifteen to eighteen feet long and nine feet wide) over the boats. Nail them securely over the edges. Take all spare oars off the outside of the boats. Lash them right, lengthwise, down the middle of the cargo. Attend to the fastenings at bow and stern. All men to the pans and bail!"

I found myself with the men, bailing, bailing, bailing. Heavens! how the water found, and lodged in, the hollows. Despite the great seamanship of the men, I feared we would be swamped. Now I understood the wisdom of Bruce's command, "towich!" Out here on the open water, the waves were less treacherous than inshore. They were longer and heavier, more like sea waves.

Nearer shore, the backwash would have swamped the boat.

It seems like yesterday that I was set in that stormy scene. The bitter oaths of the men punctuated the bellowing wind as the heavy combers struck the boat fore and aft, reared over the bow, and drenched us to the skin.

"Bail, bail!" Bruce's voice never ceased. The pitch-black night wore on. No man hesitated. Not one complained. The cold was a knife cutting into us like pain. No matter! Through the thumping seas, the men remained strong and steady in their rowing places. They were galley slaves; Bruce, their master. I sometimes wonder if there are men anywhere today—men of the breed of these Red River voyageurs.

Out of the long, nervous hours a grey dawn came. At the helm, Bruce was a Viking of old come to life, standing his boat to the open sea. I wished that morning that I were an artist to paint him so—the great pilot, his muscles like whipcords alive on his brown body. The men broke into song—great, joyous, lusty song. They had forgotten their thirst, their fatigue. They were triumphant.

I had forgotten about my personal servant. We had had little food or rest for three days. Our lives and the cargo were in peril. From the mouth of the Red to Berens River, a distance of 150 miles, we never went ashore. We made a record trip of 300 miles to Norway House in three days. This was the first lap of our journey to Mackenzie's river. The fresh-water brand of seamanship of the Red River boatmen is no legend. Some years later, it took me twenty-one days to make this trip.

The boatmen, handling heavy sweeps twenty feet long, had to rise to their feet with every pull on the oars and go back to a sitting position as they completed the swing. The endurance of these French-Canadian and Scottish boatmen, toiling at the sweeps hour after hour through hot days and cold, cannot be described. It was the bowman's duty to guide the boats through fast water and fend off rocks with a long pole. The steersman controlled the boat's direction with a sweep fastened to the stern. A senior steersman or guide usually commanded a brigade of York boats. A square sail was carried to take advantage of a favourable wind on any lake or open water.

In addition to sail, each boat was provided with three duck covers, kettles, frying pans, axe, hammer, a tool chest, ropes for hauling the boat over the portage on rollers, and lighter ropes for tracking against wind and current.

From the breakup of ice in the spring to the freeze-up in the fall, these boats were moving on the waterways of the Mackenzie, the Saskatchewan, and Red rivers. They were the arteries of the fur trade.

CHAPTER 4

I Reach Norway House

At Norway House we (the Red River brigade) put off and took on cargo. We left here American-made goods, consisting chiefly of clothing, iron works, cottons, shoes—mostly supplies which the northern posts had neglected to order from England and which the Fort Garry post had brought in from St. Paul. There was a good deal of trade carried on between the Fort Garry post and the United States, the goods being transported in winter by ox sleds, four or six to a sled, and in summer by steamboat. Everything we got from the States, however, was of secondary quality: American sugar was poor, their flour cheap. None of it could compare with the goods brought from England. But of course the Hudson's Bay prided itself on carrying only first-class merchandise.

We left at Norway House, including missionary property, half our cargo—about four or five tons. I remember there were a hundred or a couple of hundred, hundred-pound sacks of cheap American flour. Two days was the average time allowed for business at this post.

We took on board here goods which had been in winter store at this post for Mackenzie's river. It took just four years for the Mackenzie River District to get goods from England. This meant that it was necessary for the officers of this district to indent[3] for supplies four years in advance of the time they would be required. For instance, their orders took a year to reach York Factory, another year to get to England. This order was filled and shipped from England to York Factory the following year. From there it got as far as Oxford House or Cumberland House, where it was put in winter store. The next year it arrived at Fort Simpson and thence to the posts on Mackenzie's river. Goods for the Yukon wintered in the Mackenzie's river, going on to their destination the following summer.

On the fifth year, the outfit was subdivided and sent to the different posts, each one getting its quota. These goods were in turn traded to the Indians for furs which were shipped in the following spring via Mackenzie River brigade to York Factory, thence to England, where they were put on the London fur market and cash realised, cash which the Company had invested six years earlier. A complete transaction occupied six years: a year for the order to reach York (from the interior), another year for it to get to England, a year for the order to be shipped from England, and so on.

There was no other business in the world then, or perhaps yet, to compare with this: three complete outfits lying dead along the road. A great many people abused the Company for its methods of business, but they knew nothing about it. And again, those highly coloured statements about the Company giving excessive amounts of liquor to the Indians—all this is foolishness and exaggeration.

The post managers realized their responsibility in giving rum to Indians. They couldn't afford to take chances on having their posts destroyed by excited Indians, their valuable goods pillaged, and their own lives and interests endangered. Rum was not considered in the active trade. Rum was to buy goodwill.

In checking with the second officer the inventories of goods held in winter storage at Norway House, I remarked that we put a good deal of goods off for the missionaries, who must be thriving.

"That's neither here nor there, so far as the Company is concerned," said he. "We are a commercial fur-trading corporation. We attend to the bodily wants of the Indians only, apart from trading with them."

Well, I was a mischievous sort of fellow and, seeing that this chief clerk took himself so seriously, I asked, "You leave the souls of the Indians entirely to the care of themselves and the missionaries, then?"

"We never interfere with their fads, superstitions, or beliefs," he said, spreading out his lists. I felt properly rebuked and we got on with the business at hand.

A little later in chatting with James McDougall, the junior clerk in charge of the store, I said, "Your chief clerk seemed dashed touchy when I spoke about the Company being paternal and that sort of thing to the natives."

McDougall laughed. "Yes, he is touchy, rather. He is unmarried, legally, but he has an Indian wife and family. He is the son of a chief factor and he was brought up in the country. He is not so bound by the strict rules that apply to clerks as we are. He can marry legally, if he wishes."

McDougall was a young recruit who had wintered at the post in order to proceed with the summer brigade to Mackenzie's river. "I suppose you mean," I said, "that a recruit must be single, physically fit, age twenty to twenty-five, before being sent North on a five-year contract?"

"Yes," he said, "there are obstacles to prevent clerks from marrying. Accommodation for married folk at the posts is limited. Still, even if the rules are strict, they are elastic. If an engaged servant wishes to keep an Indian common law wife *pro tem*, this is allowed, providing she is kept outside the Company's grounds and he doesn't cause public scandal."

"What is the outcome of these irregular unions?" I asked.

"Improving the breed of the natives. The women look forward to having healthy children who will help them in their old age. The Company recognizes that half-breed youths make able hunters, unparalleled boatmen, and dependable temporary servants. These youths are well regarded by the Company."

I knew that the Company had established a law in regard to these alliances and required it to be observed to the last letter. When an officer having a common-law Indian wife was transferred to another post, the Company insisted that he provide for this wife and her children.

"These alliances bother the missionaries, I suppose?" I said.

"Yes, but they do the best they can. Their influence at the posts is felt," said McDougall.

Young James McDougall seemed fated for tragedy. He went on the Yukon post and in 1865, a clerk named Cowley, son of Archdeacon Cowley, Missionary at St. Peters in the Selkirk Colony, was sent to serve under him. Young Cowley had been at Sandhurst Military College, but did not finish.

At the breakup of ice that spring, McDougall took Cowley out to hunt geese and, running short of ammunition, he sent the lad back to the fort across the river for more. Cowley and a young Scotsman started back across the rotting ice, dragging an old leaky canoe. In open water the canoe swamped.

McDougall saw Cowley try to save his companion, but they were both swept under the ice. McDougall was a perfect athlete and a powerful swimmer, often swimming the river at Fort Simpson, which was a mile or more wide, but he was obliged to watch the tragedy, powerless to help. The bodies of the youths were found a year later.

Soon after this accident, McDougall went out after geese again, taking a young Indian boy. He sat in the boat reading, waiting for a flight. Suddenly the boy said, "Geese!"

McDougall grabbed his gun. The trigger caught and the gun went off, shooting the head off the boy. These accidents preyed on McDougall's mind so seriously that he asked Chief Factor Hardisty to transfer him from the Yukon post.

While we were at Norway House a party of native hunters came to the store with furs. Some spoke Cree, others Ojibway, French, and English. The chief clerk was fluent in all these languages. Languages were a necessity in the North, as I'd soon learn, he said. These native-born clerks were clever, fine fellows. They possessed the confidence of their people and, as they knew furs, they were valuable to the Company.

Three official dances and a good deal of card playing kept us entertained during our stay at Norway House. On the evening of our second day, Baptiste Bruce gave his call—*embarque!*—and we were off. Reverend George McDougall, who had charge of the Methodist mission at Playgreen Lake, brought his school children to see us off. Poor fellow, he was frozen to death on the prairie some years later.

We moved away from Norway House with the voices of the boatmen rising above the fiddle as it went from one man to another, each playing his favourite tune.

Soon our boats were caught in a light, fair wind. Bruce ran up the sails and the crew rested on their oars. We were carried rapidly up Jackfish Lake to what was afterwards known as Warren's Landing, an outlet of Lake Winnipeg, but later we were delayed over half a day by stubborn winds.

Bruce soon established a proper travelling schedule and strict discipline. Our brigade was at last heading for Mackenzie's river. Grand Rapids post would be our next stopping place.

Round a sharp bend in the river we met rapids. I was standing beside Bruce when our boat shot around an elbow in the river and I saw the white churning water.

"This one is bad," said Bruce. He commanded his men to head the boat sharply to shore. Here he assigned sixteen men—the crews of two boats—to his own, the boat we were in. Four of these men he left on shore to handle the tracking lines. He left me with them.

Bruce got into his boat with the other twelve men, took the helm, and struck out for the center of the channel. As the boat darted away, the trackers on shore slackened their lines, then hauled, slackened again, steadying the boat as it advanced. One man lost his foothold on the slippery rocks and fell into the vicious rapids, then another went in. I lent a hand in rescuing them. They were great swimmers, but it was all we could do to save them. Over the years, these rapids had taken the lives of many great boatmen.

The half-drowned trackers threw off their wet clothes, took a spot of rum, and were as fit as ever. Bruce and his men were making steady headway through the rapids with the precious cargo. At a shallow place they were hauling the boat over rocks. At a point a mile ahead, Bruce would land the cargo. There the *real* portage would begin.

Under the relentless Bruce, the boats were taken safely over the rapids and the boatmen started to portage the cargo. The rapids here extended for nine miles but by tracking the smaller rapids we reduced the portage to six.

When I surveyed the tremendous undertaking that faced the

men, the transportation of eighty thousand pounds—eight hundred pieces of one hundred pounds each—on men's backs in two days, I said to Bruce, "It can't be done! This is a backbreaking job." He laughed and said, "The men know their work. Two days for this job. No longer. We work on schedule time!"

Past the portage, we sailed when the wind was suitable, tracked along the rivers and rowed, according to the nature of our watercourse. The men's first choice was sailing, then poling, next rowing, and lastly tracking. Tracking was exhausting work. The men walked along the shore and, with carrying straps which were placed over their foreheads and attached to lines fastened to the main towing ropes, pulled or hauled the boat upstream. Generally there were four men to a tracking line.

In the rivers, the steersman steered with a long oar called a sweep; in other places he used a rudder. The masts, when not in use, were rolled up, tied, and swung outside and alongside the gunwale of the boat, above the water. Spare oars, yard, and rigging were folded into a neat bundle. On the opposite side of the boat a bundle of extra poles, twelve feet long and as stout as a man's wrist, were slung. These poles were for emergencies.

We went rapidly along. Bruce and the matchless boatmen under his command worked in perfect harmony. Then, suddenly, the brigade hove in view of the Company's post at Grand Rapids. We were greeted with a salute of guns and mighty cheering.

CHAPTER 5

Grand Rapids to Portage La Loche

The Grand Rapids post was only a temporary transport or receiving station. It had four buildings: a trading shop; a depot for storing goods at the time of transfer of cargoes; a small house for clerks; and a larger one for the men. It was only during the summer when the brigades were moving that there was a permanent clerk in charge. Then it became a place of colour and activity. The chief officer who accompanied the brigades took charge of the business. Here, as at all posts, mails were delivered, letters answered, cargoes put off. The boats were turned over to the boat builders to be overhauled, freshly tarred, blazed, and oakum which had come out of the seams replaced. The boats got knocked about badly when they were hauled over the rapids.

Chief Factor Pierre Deschambault was the officer in charge of the Grand Rapids District. This district was extensive. It had flying posts and outposts, temporary places for traders and runners to meet and collect furs from the Indian hunters. We had met Deschambault at Horse Island, which is opposite Montreal Island, on our way to Grand Rapids. He was bound for York Factory. He was an odd looking man. He flailed his hands about when he spoke and had a strong French accent. He had an interesting personality, was a capable officer, and greatly appreciated by the Company. I never knew an officer who, when business was down, could cut expenses so cleverly without impairing efficiency. I got to know him well in later years.

The Indians at the post were busy fishing. The men were naked except for breechclouts. The boatmen engaged these people to help them portage their cargoes, paying them out of their own pockets at the rate of two shillings for a ninety- to one-hundred-pound package. Four shillings was the rate paid for a load of two hundred pounds. Often the men paid in clothes—an extra pair of trousers or a shirt. The women could carry as much as the men. It was nothing to see a woman swinging along the trail with a hundred-pound package slung across her shoulders and a baby on top of it. When she wanted to spell, she would lean against a tree—it was too much bother to unload—get her breath and go on. It was a knack to load the packages: the carrier would hold a carrying strap between his teeth, grasp the package with his hands, and swing it over his head.

Two days from the Grand Rapids post, after minor delays when the cargo had to be portaged over rapids, our brigade touched Cedar Lake. This was not a regular post but a fishing station with a Métis engaged servant in charge. It was attached to Moose Lake post, Cumberland District, which was under Chief Factor Roderick Mackenzie, nicknamed Red Roderick. The Company maintained fishing stations along the Mackenzie River route. We visited several on our way.

At one end of Cedar Lake, we came upon amber deposits and Bruce took me to examine them. I made up my mind that if ever I were stationed here, I would do some prospecting.

Some years later, in 1884–86, when I was in charge of the Moose Lake post, at a place called Chemahawin (Cree for seining ground), which was near the post, Mr. MacFarlane and I collected, in three years, over a thousand pounds of beautiful amber. I sent a specimen to Thomas Edison, the inventor. He wrote back advising us to disregard the amber and look for gold. We personally paid for the work. Donald A. Smith, later Lord Strathcona, offered to privately finance our work, but we had no time or wish to engage in a private business venture.

From Cedar Lake to The Pas and on to Cumberland House, where we left the Saskatchewan River, our route was through the celebrated muskrat swamps of western Canada. In this region muskrats then swarmed in millions. At the Cedar Lake and Cumberland posts we took in trade, annually, over a quarter of a million muskrats. The average price for a pelt was ten cents—that was about twenty-five thousand dollars for muskrats alone. Other furs taken in this district were otter, mink, beaver, fisher, and bear. It was a great country, which was teeming with fur-bearing animals!

The Pas was just a small trading outpost in charge of Ishiah Buck, a shrewd, engaging fellow, whose name was borne with pride by the Indian chief in the region.

Seining for sturgeon was an important industry at The Pas. I was on the shore, I remember, watching the men at work when a boatman put a line into my hand and asked me to pull. I hauled out a huge sturgeon. This was a joke the men played on greenhorns. The live sturgeon had been tethered. This was a novel Indian way of keeping fish fresh. One end of a ten-foot line was run through the tail of the fish, the other pegged to a stake on shore. If the line was too short, the fish drowned; if too long, it got tangled. Fish could be kept alive in this way for two or three days. In netting fish, one end of the net was picketed to the bank, the other anchored in the river. Sturgeon weighed up to two hundred pounds; the catches here were enormous.

Cumberland House, which we presently reached, was built for the Company by Samuel Hearne in 1774 on Pine Island (now Cumberland Lake) and was the first Hudson's Bay post in the interior. Prior to 1870, all the pemmican for provisioning the brigades—thousands of bags—was stored here.

Over the Sturgeon River we went to join the English River (now known as Churchill) at Stanley. To reach it we had to cross Frog Portage. This was a tricky place. A great ledge of rocks, 150 yards wide, extended from water to water, sending one-half into Lake Winnipeg, the other into Hudson Bay at Fort Nelson. Even at high water, this ledge rises to about ten feet above the surface. These rocks could be dynamited and the water diverted into Lake Winnipeg. At this portage, we unloaded everything and hauled our boats across those terrible ledges. From this point on, all the travel was upstream.

From Stanley to Ile-à-la-Crosse, we found the territory overrun with porcupines. They were plentiful in this region. The porcupine feeds at night on the bark of young poplars, not on grass, as many think. Its flesh is good—like pork—and I have eaten many porcupines. It is a peculiar and quiet little animal. Boatmen could go right up to them and knock them on the head. Porcupines were a curiosity to the new Red River men.

As we travelled the men caught fish at the rapids, sometimes in nets, but generally by scooping. The English River is the most celebrated river in the Northwest for scooping fish, the heavy white fish.

Time was everything. We travelled on Sundays and in the heaviest weather. When possible, we camped ashore at night. We started at daylight. Bruce was the first one up mornings—and his loud *leve, leve! Il faut partir!* soon got us astir. His job was to make the fire. The men collected the wood, the camp attendant boiled the kettle and cooked breakfast: a cup of tea, bannock, and a bit of pemmican for Bruce and myself. Each man prepared his own breakfast of tea, pemmican, and bannock if he had one made, or pemmican and water. Pemmican was handy. It did not require cooking.

After breakfast, Bruce called *embarque!* and jumped into his boat. The bowman untied the boat, lit his pipe, and pushed off; those who weren't ready had to run or jump for the boat. The other boats had to catch up with us as best they could. Bruce didn't bother about them. He wouldn't stop for anything. An hour was allowed from the minute we put ashore for breakfast until we shoved off again. A fellow who hadn't got his breakfast in that time was out of luck. The men never complained.

A young man's greatest ambition in those days was to get a job on a York Factory boat. The requirements were boat experience, good health, strength, and reliability. An accepted applicant had to sign a witnessed contract at Fort Garry. It was distinctly expressed in the contract that a man engaged for the trip with the Red River brigade had to travel to Norway House, to Portage La Loche, back to Norway House, down to York Factory, and back to Fort Garry. The length of the trip was estimated at three months, more or less.

It was like getting the Victoria Cross to be accepted into the

Red River brigade. Competition was keen amongst the guides to secure the best boatmen available. Each guide had to engage his boatmen subject to the approval of the Company.

The next post of our route was Ile-à-la-Crosse. This was the separating point between ancient and modern freighting. At one time all the Company freight went over this route. Later, in 1880, a change of routes took place—the boats forked off across Green Lake, where the cargoes left water by way of land to Prince Albert, thence by steamboat down the Saskatchewan River to Lake Winnipeg. The old route was not completely abandoned, but this change marked the turning point in transportation routes for the Hudson's Bay Company.

Samuel Mackenzie, who was temporarily in charge of the Ile-à-la-Crosse post, took us to his home for tea, served in a lovely garden walled in by a white picket fence. It reminded me of an English garden with its profusion of flowers and vines. We had tea, cakes, wine, and wild jam. Mackenzie had three charming daughters who had been educated in Montreal. They could speak several languages and play the harmonica and concertina. They were dressed as fine as any girl in good English society.

Bishop Taché had a Catholic mission here, the farthest north at this time. I had known Bishop Taché (afterwards archbishop) at St. Boniface. He was a wonderful man. He used to say to John McTavish, Hargrave, and myself—all the young fellows going to the native dances—"Go, enjoy yourselves, but take God with you!" There was fun in his eye and a great righteousness which the young clerks, though not of his faith, heeded.

From Ile-à-la-Crosse on, we were in a different country. We went by way of Beaver Lake into Portage La Loche River. Beaver Lake is celebrated for storms that sweep over it with terrific suddenness, making it extremely dangerous in winter as well as in summer. It is a small basin-like lake, surrounded by high hills. The Indians named it, suitably, "Lake of the Winds." The brigades always dreaded crossing Beaver Lake.

The Company never lost boats on this lake, but there were constant mishaps amongst the Indians who travelled it in canoes. In the La Loche River there were three celebrated rocky portages, the longest being nearly a mile.

The La Loche River took us to Cedar Lake from which we

branched into a narrow three-mile creek that ended at the foot of Portage La Loche. In places this creek was so cramped that we had to channel a passage for our boats. Once out, we made for Portage La Loche—(the long portage) with all speed. This was the turning point of the Red River brigade.

It was very important that all the brigades—those from Athabaska, Carlton, Cumberland House, Ile-à-la-Crosse, and Mackenzie River—meet at Portage La Loche on or about the 10th of July and exchange cargoes. Not all the brigades went to York Factory—only those east of Portage La Loche. The others went back the way they had come, with goods instead of furs. We went north with the Mackenzie River brigade.

The 14th of August was the time the ship generally arrived from England to take on a cargo of furs. It was especially important that the Athabaska brigade (three boats known as the summer brigade), which was the farthest away, meet the Mackenzie River brigade at Portage La Loche, exchange cargoes, join our brigade, and go on to Norway House. If it missed the English ship, the furs it brought would have to remain in the country until the next year.

Portage La Loche is the height of land separating the waters flowing into the Arctic from those running down the Saskatchewan River into Hudson Bay. Here we met the Mackenzie River outfit. Halfway across the twelve-mile portage our carriers (six men out of a boat crew of eight) met those from the Mackenzie River brigade and exchanged cargoes. So perfectly timed was the meeting of these brigades that, no matter what the weather, neither one was more than a few days beyond the scheduled time. This was very important, as the posts were only provisioned for a definite period.

On landing, our crew had to climb a six-hundred-foot hill that seemed almost perpendicular, through scrub and sand. The road was fairly well cut out; still it was a tremendous task. The entire cargo was carried to the top of this hill, each carrier making two trips in a half day.

Bruce now divided the cargo evenly among the carriers. Two men from each boat (who were not carriers) were detailed to help the carriers load their packages. Bruce went ahead to check the loads brought by the Mackenzie River carriers and keep the packages from getting mixed with those from our own outfit.

Each carrier made two trips across the six miles in a half day. To exchange the entire cargo each carrier had to make six to eight trips across the portage, carrying a load each way. A fur pack, though bulky, did not weigh more than seventy-five or a hundred pounds. These packages were slung from the carrier's forehead by a portage strap, one piece being placed lengthwise across his shoulders, for balance; the other crosswise. The weight was borne by his forehead. The weight allowance for each carrier was two hundred pounds, but some of these boatmen could carry three or four hundred pounds apiece. This amount was not required of them, however. It was their own choice. The Red River boatmen had it pretty hard. It took a week to transfer this cargo—on men's backs.

The cargoes were transported in military style. Each package had to be accounted for and each carrier was responsible for the transportation of his own packs. If he was unable to carry his packs, he had to pay someone to carry them for him. Wherever the packages were deposited, a man was detailed to guard them.

From Portage La Loche to York Factory, Baptiste Bruce and L'Esperance had the responsibility of the Mackenzie River annual outfits of furs valued at between thirty thousand dollars and fifty thousand dollars. The Mackenzie and Athabaska rivers were the backbone of the fur trade. To this important trade district, the Company always assigned their best men.

CHAPTER 6

With the Mackenzie River Brigade

I set off in high spirits with the Mackenzie River brigade. Under different names, Mackenzie's river runs from the Rocky Mountains, by the Athabaska and Slave, to the Arctic, or from British Columbia by the Peace. It drains most of the northern half of the continent and has as great a mileage as the Amazon.

The Mackenzie River boats were larger than those of the Red River, having a thirty-five to thirty-six foot keel and a ten to eleven foot beam. They were manned by ten men; the cargo load was 125 packages of one hundred pounds weight to each boat. These boats did not draw much more water than the smaller ones, but they were more suitable for the immense northern lakes—especially Great Slave Lake, which is one of the largest lakes on the American continent.

Though the distance from Portage La Loche to Fort Simpson was considerably more than that from Fort Garry to Portage La Loche, we could, on the up grade—that is going upstream—make it in about half the time and downstream in a quarter of the time.

We went down the Clearwater River to the forks of the Athabaska at Fort McMurray. (The map will contradict this. The Fort McMurray we visited was situated at the fork of the Clearwater and the Athabaska. It was built at the junction of the rivers for the accommodation of the water transport.) The Company had brought cattle from Edmonton to winter at this post for use in transporting cargoes over the portage. The post was on a bank forty feet above water.

In the spring of 1873, when I was at Fort Chipewyan, an ice jam at the forks raised the water to sixty feet, drowning the cattle, and destroying the fort and the stables. The Company couldn't risk rebuilding a fort on the old site, so under the direction of Chief Factor William McMurray, a new one was put up twelve miles down the river. It was one of the great posts of the Company. The present Fort McMurray, however, stands on the old site.

The flood of 1873 demoralized the transport. Men now refused to carry loads on their backs and demanded cattle to haul the cargoes. A new era of transportation had begun.

Harry Moberly was in charge of Fort McMurray at the time of its destruction and without waiting for orders, he drove posthaste to Edmonton and brought more cattle to transport the cargoes. For this quality of leadership, he was promoted from clerk to chief trader, a promotion of two steps, which was unusual in the service. But for his forethought and leadership, the extensive Mackenzie River District would have been without supplies for a whole year.

On the other side of the river at Fort McMurray, on the main Athabaska, we came to the celebrated tar sands. Here the country was saturated with tar pools. Oil lay on the surface and black tar oozed from the riverbanks. It could be smelled for miles. Tar from this region was used for caulking boats and for tarring house roofs. The natives used this spongy tar-soaked earth for fuel. In travelling through these tar-banked rivers, we carried empty casks and the men scraped moss from the tar beds and let the tar seep into the kegs until they were a third full, adding a little water to each keg to prevent the tar from swelling, which it did in hot weather.

A tar mixture for roofs was prepared by boiling tar with grease or spruce gum. This gummy mixture made a fine, smooth finish for the almost flat house roofs, upon which quantities of meat were dried. Peter Pond mentions these tar sands in his 1788 diary. When John Macoun, the geologist, stayed at my post in 1875, he made a report to Ottawa about the quantity of tar available in this region.

We made three portages on our way, to avoid the rapids: *la pain*, the Bread Portage; *la brulé*, the Burnt Wood Portage; and *la sulph*, the Sulphur Springs Portage.

We were two days going from Fort McMurray to Fort Chipewyan, a distance of 190 miles. On this downward trip, our north brigade travelled as much as possible at night. The crew tied the three boats together, sideways—an oar fastened between them—allowing them to drift. Two men sat in the middle boat, steering. We generally made five or six miles an hour, drifting.

The most important rapid we met between the swift portage on the Clearwater and Fort Chipewyan was the one at Mountain Portage. This fall, more than twenty feet perpendicular, poured into the river, which was nearly three-quarters of a mile wide—a Niagara on a small scale. The ordinary rate of the current on the Athabaska River is from three and a half to four miles an hour. Mountain Portage was at the end of navigation for brigades from Fort Chipewyan and Fort Simpson. No navigation could mount it. In later years, we built steamers that ran from Fort McMurray to Fort Fitzgerald right at the upper end of the Mountain Portage. Now a road crosses this gap. The length of the Mountain Portage was sixteen miles.

The Athabaska steamer *Grahame*—named after Commissioner James A. Grahame—was the first steamer built (1884). The next was the *Wrigley*, named after Commissioner Joseph Wrigley.

It took us two days to unload our boats at Fort Chipewyan and make out new bills of lading and take on over-supplies for Fort Simpson. We put the packages for distribution at posts along our route into one boat, our own supplies into another.

When I went to Fort Chipewyan some years later, second to Roderick Ross MacFarlane, we used Point La Brea for a fishing base. Our engaged servants fished there regularly. We established three fisheries: one at Point La Brea; one opposite Fort Chipewyan—six miles across the lake at Claire; the third at the entry to Slave River. We called this the Rapid River Fishery.

La Brea was a disputed word in my day. Some claimed that it was French for shelter; others that it meant tar point. We thought this curious as there wasn't any tar there.

We called the island, four miles opposite Fort Chipewyan, Calf

Island. We kept young calves on it, to protect them from wild animals, about twenty head of cattle, and half a dozen horses. Before my time, as many as forty head were pastured on the island. The horses were imported from England. We also kept a man on Potato Island to raise potatoes and vegetables. Once the priest Père Clut, afterwards Bishop Clut, sent wheat to the World's Fair in Chicago and won a prize. He had a patch, about an acre, of wheat that he nursed along, lighting fires around it on cold nights to prevent frosts.

The original Fort Chipewyan, built by Roderick McKenzie of the North West Company, on Old Fort Point, about twenty miles from the present post, was gone. Only the foundations and the chimneys remained. The post had been rebuilt twice since McKenzie's time, neither time on the original site. An opposition fort was built six miles from here by the X Y Company, but it was absorbed by the North West Company in 1804. Only a shell remained of this old building. Fort Wedderburn was built on Potato Island by the Hudson's Bay Company, but sometime after 1820 it was deserted and Chipewyan became its headquarters. Potato Island was chosen out of the chain of islands that protected Fort Chipewyan from the lake and against attacks from opposition traders.

From Fort Chipewyan Chief Trader W. L. Hardisty was in charge of the brigade. Two hundred miles downstream we came to Fort Resolution. This was a big post and a celebrated place. A post was first built here by the North West Company. Their rivals, the Hudson's Bay Company, put up a post within three or four miles of it and named it Fort Resolution. When I first saw the place, on this trip, only the cellars and the stonework of the old North West Company post were left. One of my men, Louis Cadien, who had been an Indian runner for the post, gave me a good deal of information about it. He used to be sent out with trading goods to the Indian hunting grounds and settlements in opposition to other posts and their runners.

At Fort Resolution we left the Slave River and went across Great Slave Lake to Fort Providence. We started with a fair wind, which gradually lifted and broke into a terrific storm. We had to lower our sails, leaving only enough sail to allow steering way on the boats. We made shelter north of Hay River until the storm was over, then continued to Fort Providence, where there was a place to dry our wet cargo.

Now we were on the main Mackenzie River! This is a great river. From the edge of the banks on each side stretched a well-timbered forest. And here was a sight for our tired eyes: the forests right down to the water on both sides were on fire.

Fortunately, the wind was strong and blowing down the river. Smoke from the flames joined above us, forming an archway. We had to sail under this burning archway for three or four miles, in great danger. We carried sixteen forty-pound kegs of gunpowder in each of our three boats. We lashed all available coverings over the cargoes, including our clothing and blankets. Ten men sat on the side of each boat, dipping water out of the river and pouring it over the sparks, cinders, burning branches, and hot ashes that fell upon us. It was a terrible experience, moving slowly under that flaming arch and through the acrid smoke that dried our throats. If the flames should reach our gunpowder it meant death to us all. This gunpowder, too, meant life and death to the men at the Mackenzie River posts. At length we got past the flaming canopy and were safe.

We proceeded, travelling day and night. About ninety miles downstream from Fort Providence we encountered a very strong current. This was called the head of the line because it was here that the up-going crews had to track the boats with a line. For two days on the way upstream the men had to track this current for sixty miles. The stones on the floor of the deep channel here were kept constantly rolling by the current. The swish of the water caused by these rolling stones sounded like the noise of a rapid. Normally the current in the river proper runs about five miles an hour.

At last we came within sight of Fort Simpson. This fort is situated on an island at the junction of the Liard and Mackenzie's rivers. About twelve miles out we got a long straight view of it. The waters meet at this junction to form one great river two or three miles wide. This river continues to the Arctic Ocean. This is one thousand miles of river—north.

Opposite Rabbit Skin River, where our brigade could be seen from the fort, we halted and Baptiste Bouvier, the guide, changed the positions of the crews. He put the picked boatmen in his own boat and gave them new sweaters so they would be uniformly dressed. The flag of the Company was run up. The men got their guns loaded and placed at hand, ready to answer the salute from the fort. The chief singers in the brigade were instructed to lead the singing when the boats should near the fort.

The crews joined in the singing and through their songs ran all the joy of their achievement and safe arrival—three months of travel up rivers, across rapids, over backbreaking portages, across the dangerous Great Slave and Athabaska lakes. They had fought storms and strong currents and safely transported valuable fur returns and merchandise of all kinds. They carried life to the district.

The race over the last quarter-mile stretch to the fort was exciting and we landed in approved military fashion. Chief Trader Hardisty and Baptiste Bouvier were the first to land.

As soon as they set foot onshore, the crew began carrying the cargo to the depot, where it was received by the fort clerks. The steersmen assisted with this work, piling the bales, cases, kegs, and bags so that the marks on them were visible and legible. The gunpowder was taken to the powder magazine, which was situated at a safe distance from other buildings.

Immediately after the unloading was finished, the boats were dispatched to the carpenter shop to be repaired and tarred for their trip with cargoes to the lower posts—Fort Norman, Fort Good Hope, Peel's river, Rampart House, and Fort Yukon.

When the cargoes were unloaded, each boatman was given the usual regale of well-diluted rum and his rations. The customary supper and dance was held. The crews got out their fiddles, tambourines, and drums and provided the music. The dance, as was customary, was opened by the chief factor and his wife.

Early next morning, each clerk was given a particular job. The brigades must be ready to leave in three or four days. Nothing must delay the Lower Mackenzie boats. The season was shortening, the journey long. They must be off before they were caught in snow and ice. Packs were opened, unpacked, repacked. Supplies were got ready for the wintering inland servants, clerks, and missionaries. The boatmen were paid. The Company never kept discontented men. They injured the business. This was especially true of the Mackenzie River District. In the frontier districts, which ran from Ile-à-la-Crosse to Lesser Slave Lake, and included Edmonton and Carlton, men were frequently changed. But for the important Mackenzie River District a special class were picked. They were not changed often and when they were, they considered it a grievance.

Now the brigades were broken up and re-formed. The boats of the down brigade, those going north to the lower posts, started first. These posts were cut off from civilization for a year. There was only a down packet once a year, in winter, and the second packet by open water with the boats. Naturally, the cargoes had to be carefully and correctly supervised. There would be no chance to repair shortages or mistakes within the year.

The three boats of the down brigade were manned by Indians from their respective posts. The boatmen from Yukon and Peel's river had to finish their trip on snowshoes. Each man carried forty pounds besides his own provisions and blankets. In payment for this work he received forty skins.

The cargo for the Yukon was first taken, in this way, to Peel's river, then overland—over the portage by dog train—a distance of around a hundred miles. From there it was taken down the Porcupine River to Fort Yukon. The cargoes from Fort Simpson reached Peel's river at the end of October. It was well towards the middle of November before goods reached the Yukon post. Always in this story I mean Old Fort Yukon, which was in what was then Russian territory. At the Yukon post a small dance was given, a small affair in comparison to the one given at Fort Simpson.

The departure of the down brigade was followed by the others; the Fort Liard boat on the west branch of Mackenzie's river, a distance of 150 miles, more or less; the Fort Providence boat on the east Mackenzie. The Fort Resolution boat, on Great Slave Lake, and the Fort Rae boat, on the northeast end of Great Slave Lake, were the last to be outfitted and sent out. The boats couldn't be held.

From Fort Simpson, the chief factor placed me in charge of two boats, one heading for Fort Rae, the other for Fort Providence. A third boat that had been sent to the post for the fall fishing accompanied us as far as Fort Providence. We were fifteen days making Fort Rae, a distance of three hundred miles upstream on Mackenzie's river and two hundred across Great

Slave Lake. It was the time for the autumn storms on Great Slave Lake, but we were fortunate enough to escape any serious ones.

Well, here I was in the Mackenzie River District, attached to Fort Rae and committed to life in the sub-Arctic, thousands of miles from civilization, where each post manager looked at his instructions for the year and carried on. His companions were three or four white engaged servants, as many temporary engaged native servants, and the Indian tribes. I must say that the officers living at the widely separated posts in this far region appeared loyal and contented. Some of them had been in Mackenzie River for ten or twelve years, some for a lifetime. Our main living here consisted of whatever the region produced. We had fish of many kinds, migratory birds, moose, caribou, muskox, beaver, muskrat, and a small allowance of so-called luxuries—flour, tea, and sugar. We did not feel too sorry for ourselves.

When I entered the service there was no tea imported for trade. The Company made a small allowance to each post for the officers and a little for the boats. For the whole district (twelve posts) two and a half chests of tea were allotted for special occasions. A clerk's tea allowance was fifteen pounds a year; a commanding officer got twenty pounds; for the post the limit was ten pounds. This was for the mess table when brigades arrived and clerks came from all over. That brings me to sugar: two kegs of sugar a year were allowed the whole district for trading purposes. This was not sold but a little was given to Indian chiefs or headmen when they came to trade or came from far places. An apprentice's allowance was sixty pounds a year; a commissioned officer got double this amount (two kegs); clerks were given as much as an apprentice. The sugar came packed in long bars, elongated pyramids—we called them *touques* or sugar loaves. Three of these filled a barrel. In the space between, lump sugar was packed to keep the bars solid. Each of these touques weighed from eight to ten pounds.

The yearly allowance for flour for the whole district for trading purposes was four bags. This was for regales for men and for entertaining officers when they came to the depot. An apprentice clerk was allowed one bag (ninety-eight pounds) 3X flour a year; a clerk, two bags; an officer, three bags. The four bags allotted to the depot were for running the mess in the summer when brigades came from all over. The total amount of flour shipped into Mackenzie River—thirteen posts—was from eighty to one hundred bags of flour a year.

We had two kinds of imported rolled tobacco. Each roll weighed sixty pounds and was as thick as a man's thumb. Then we had tobacco—eighteen plugs to the pound. This was imported by the Company in shiploads direct from the West Indies. We had a great tobacco trade. If any other tobacco was brought into the country, it had to come in through an officer's private account.

We were always busy. I often regarded it as a blessing that mails arrived at the northern posts only once a year. More than a yearly mail would have interfered seriously with business. Between mails, the collecting of furs, outfitting of hunters, and running a great territory—being a sort of emperor generally— was responsibility enough for any post manager.

Speaking about the northern tribes, the Indians of my day knew the value of things. They were primitive but they were intelligent. The Eskimo were in their native state. They liked the Company men, who brought them things they desired, but it was worth an officer's life to oppose them. It is astonishing to realize that today these Eskimo have churches of various denominations all along the northern coast, financed by themselves. They also send money to the poor and destitute in England, I am told.

It was on my way to Mackenzie River in 1863 that I first met Chief Trader Robert Campbell. He was with the Athabaska brigade from Fort Chipewyan and he had his wife and children with him. Campbell, a former post manager or clerk at Pelly Banks, a Company post, was the man who first opened up the Yukon Territory for the Company. He followed the Liard River to its source, crossed the height of land to a river running north-west, which he named the Pelly River, then travelled down this river to its junction with the Lewes River. Here he established Fort Selkirk.

In August of 1852, this post was raided by a band of Chilcat Indians and all the supplies taken or destroyed. Campbell and his native servants put up a stiff fight, but they were unequal to the strength of the invaders. While struggling for the possession of an old flintlock gun it exploded. This frightened the superstitious

Chilcats, who believed Campbell possessed dangerous magic. They were afraid to kill him and his men.

When the Indians withdrew, Campbell and a native servant, Baptiste Forcier, started back for Fort Simpson in a small birch bark canoe. Without food and clothed only in shirts and trousers, they arrived at Fort Simpson in November, and at once Campbell tried to persuade Chief Factor James Anderson to provide supplies and men for a return trip to Fort Selkirk to punish the Indians who had looted the fort.

When Anderson would not agree, Campbell resolved to appeal to a higher authority and in November he started out to walk to Fort Garry, where he arrived in February 1853. This trip of three thousand miles is regarded as the longest snowshoe tramp on record. When the authorities at Fort Garry refused his request, he continued on down to St. Paul and eventually arrived in Montreal, a month after leaving Fort Garry. Here he pleaded his case personally before Sir George Simpson who, while sympathizing deeply with his motives, refused to permit him to return, but ordered him to take a furlough in Scotland.

Campbell was a highly capable officer and highly respected by his fellow workers. As usual when meeting another brigade, we stopped and exchanged letters with the Athabaska brigade. W. J. McLean (afterwards named Big Bear McLean, because in the Métis uprising in 1885 he was captured by the noted Cree chief Big Bear) was travelling with my brigade. I was amused when he and Campbell (both Scotsmen) withdrew to hold a conference, disregarding me. I was an Englishman.

I remember that Chief Factor Lewes, who was regarded as a man of great importance in the Company, had great admiration for Campbell. Lewes preceded Hardisty and Bernard R. Ross— who was one year between them—in charge of the Mackenzie River District. He had one hand off. He kept a steward, whom he required to cut his tobacco. When he discovered that the fellow was selling his tobacco to other servants, he discharged him. The steward was such a valuable and well-trained servant, however, that Lewes soon re-engaged him. When he was sixty, Lewes decided to take a second wife, marrying her according to Hudson's Bay law. He was very well off at this time. He bought a lot of land in Winnipeg, then went to England, bought a vessel, loaded it with merchandise, and sailed to Australia to trade. Arriving there, he discovered there was no demand for his goods. This venture almost ruined him. His daughters inherited his Winnipeg property, which was later sold for almost nothing. It is very valuable today.

Many amusing things happened in the North. I remember one romance. Hardisty was asked to order a wife from Fort Garry. Hardisty forwarded the request to Governor McTavish at Fort Garry.

The governor spoke to a widow who was living in the settlement about going north to marry an officer. She agreed on the condition that she be allowed to take her daughter, with the idea of getting the girl married also to a Company officer. Hudson's Bay officers were considered great catches in those days.

Governor McTavish arranged for the departure of the prospective brides with the Red River brigade. I happened to be at Fort Simpson when the brigade and the brides arrived. The prospective bridegroom was there, very eager. When he saw the girl, he wanted her and refused to marry the mother. All the young officers, including myself, fell in love with the girl. Each one of us—eleven in all—proposed to her.

The big dance arranged at the post this night was a very special one in honour of the marriage. After a few drinks each we felt a little jolly, but we were all in dead earnest about the girl. The girl couldn't make up her mind which officer she would take. She said, "Mother, you go in for money, I go in for love."

The prospective bridegroom went away, refusing to marry the widow. We sent two or three Indians to bring him back. At last, after encouraging him with quite a few drinks, about nine or ten o'clock that night, we got him safely married to the widow.

At the men's dance on the following evening all the officers proposed again to the girl. On the following day, they backed out. The poor groom had to take the two women—the one he wanted and the one he married—to Bear Lake.

Nicol Taylor put up the Bear Lake post about 1862. It was a convenient place for the fur traders to meet the outlying bands of Indians. Bear River itself was full of strong rapids—approximately sixty miles of them. The position chosen for the post was in the path of the hunters, on a point some twenty miles east of the outlet of the main lake. There was suitable timber in this region to build houses and for firewood. There were good fisheries: white fish, suckers, jackfish, and fresh water herring were abundant. Wild fruit was plentiful. It was the resting place for migratory birds.

It was the breeding place of geese, ducks, loons, northern divers, swans, pelicans, eagles, hawks of all kinds, cranes, and it was the farthest known point north for night hawks. In most years, deer (caribou) were plentiful here. The chief value of the post to the Company was as a provision post. The furs were chiefly muskox robes, white foxes, musquash, otter, wolverine, and bears.

CHAPTER 7

I Trade with the Montagnais and Yellowknives

Soon after my arrival at Fort Rae (1863), I was appointed first assistant to Chief Trader James Lockhart, the officer in charge of Fort Resolution. On the first ice Mr. Lockhart went to Fort Simpson to run the district during the absence of Chief Trader Hardisty, who had to visit the lower posts in winter. I was left in charge. It was rather unusual for an apprentice clerk to be entrusted with the management of an important fur-trading post. This was a rich fur territory. The Indian population subject to this post numbered about four hundred families. My wages were twenty-five pounds sterling a year. I appreciated the honour and liked it.

Trading with the Indians was not going smoothly. Fort Resolution belonged originally to the Athabaska District, but the officers were making an effort to transfer it to the Mackenzie River District. These districts differed in their tariff schedule and the Montagnais and Yellowknife Indians who traded at Fort Resolution would not accept a lower tariff or price for their furs. To satisfy them, Hardisty offered the Indians tributary to Fort Resolution the Athabaska tariff. There was continued argument and discontent.

In order to keep business running smoothly, I disregarded Company rules. Ordinarily, a marten skin was reckoned as half a skin, a beaver as one skin (a made beaver skin fixed the value of trading), and other prime skins in proportion. I gave the Indians, in addition to the market price, a bonus for good skins which I knew would fetch a higher price in England. This disregard of orders was to the Company's advantage. I created goodwill and interest amongst the hunters and developed trade. They brought in piles of furs. We had a profitable year. When Mr. Hardisty visited the post the next summer, he said, "You were wise. But remember you did not have my permission!" Mr. Hardisty stuck to me all his life—he was a fine, generous friend.

Life at the fort had its compensations. Everything interested me. I read the contents of the daily post journals of many years back, which had been well thumbed by my predecessors. I studied copies of the Fur Purchasing Tariff, the M. B. Skin Tariff, and the Trading Goods Tariff, and learned the prices by heart. From Louis Cadien, my interpreter, a Montagnais Indian half-breed, who spoke all the Indian languages as well as French and a little English, I learned and memorized the Indian names of the goods and the words for counting.

Louis Cadien was about eighty years of age and an interesting character. In his early days he had been a fur trader and runner for the North West Company.

November came. I received orders from Fort Simpson to go at once and take charge of Fort Rae. The clerk in charge, William Thomson Smith, had shot one of his men, Pierre Gendron. It was doubtful whether it was a murder or an accident. I set out with a party to investigate this unfortunate business.

Fort Rae, situated at the end of the northern arm of Great Slave Lake, was about 150 miles from Fort Resolution. From October to December, the main ice on Great Slave Lake is anything but safe for travelling. With few mishaps, however, we arrived safely at Fort Rae. The engaged servants, led by Smith's assistant, McNevin, a Scotsman, had arrested Smith, handcuffed him, and shipped him by dog sleigh and cariole under guard to Fort Simpson.

At Fort Simpson, Mr. Hardisty cut the prisoner's thongs and treated him the same as any other clerk. In the spring he sent him, with witnesses, to Fort Garry for trial.

As there was insufficient evidence to convict Smith, Donald Smith and Bishop Taché presented a plea of leniency and the case was dismissed. Smith was later sent to Fort Pelly, as assistant under Chief Factor Robert Campbell.

I made the best arrangements for Fort Rae that I could for the time being. I left McNevin in charge, with William Hoole as interpreter, to run the business until Mr. Strachan Jones, another clerk, should arrive to take charge. The weather was stormy and cold and the ice unsafe, but I returned to Fort Resolution none the worse for my trip.

During my absence several parties of Yellowknife Indians had brought in good loads of dried caribou hides, furs, dressed leather, and babiche. Louis Cadien, my old experienced interpreter, had managed well. He had collected some furs on account of advances given in early autumn, but for the bulk he had traded. It was not a difficult matter to post this business in my books and ledgers.

Christmas brought many Indians to visit the Roman Catholic priest, Père Gascon, to confess and pay for masses for their souls. The price of High Mass was five made beaver; low mass, three made beaver. The Montagnais tribe hunted moose, deer, beaver, and bear. The Yellowknives hunted mostly on the border of the Barren Lands, which was a fairly rich fur-bearing country. Caribou and muskox was their chief diet, plus fish and migratory birds. The Montagnais Indians were heavily built men and expert hunters. The Yellowknives were of slimmer build; they were expert caribou hunters.

During winter months the Indians usually arrived at night. They came by dog teams, in large or small parties, coming distances of from fifty to two hundred miles and bringing great sled loads of furs. Their arrival was an event. Sometimes they came to report sickness, accidents, or starvation.

We treated them with every consideration, storing their sleds for the night after they had taken off their blankets and other personal belongings. The chiefs or leaders became the guests of the interpreters or guides. Some put up with friends amongst Company employees; others were given accommodation at the Indian House, which we supplied with fuel and water, and they were given some food, tobacco, tea (if any), and sometimes a fish for each dog. Special provision was made for women and children in the party.

Chiefs or leaders were given a meal in the kitchen with the cook. When they were refreshed and in good temper, I invited these leaders into the officers' room or the Indian Hall to have a cheerful interview and a smoke and to hear about their hunting successes or troubles.

Bright and early the next morning the furs were examined, assorted, valued, and a note made for the value in made beaver given each hunter. The provisions they brought—dried meat and grease—were weighed and priced. Each Indian's account we adjusted and trade or advances were carried on without delay. The Indians seldom remained at the post more than two nights. There were very few disputes—simply give and take.

Marten and mink skins were strung in bunches of fifty; beaver and bearskins were placed flat on piles; muskrats we tied and piled in parcels of ten gross; wolves, otter, and lynx we strung by two's; foxes—graded red or cross-silver—by ten's; muskox, hung up singly; beaver-stone (i.e., castorum), per pound; meat, deer ribs dry or half dry, per count; grease per pound; tongues by the dozen; pounded dry meat by approximate pound, according to quality; white fish per dozen; trout by each; babiche by bundles or pound; deer skins valued per each, if with or without fur, as robes or coats; and also rabbit robes or coats. We transacted business by justice, kindness, and the regular tariffs.

In the autumn before the hunters left for the wintering hunting grounds we gave them the necessary advances and a general dinner and a dance—Indian and modern style. There were speeches, lots of noise, and some gambling. We liked to see them happy and carefree, knowing the hardships before them.

Each district post had to keep in duplicate a detailed daily account of all transactions: weather, temperature, arrivals of packets from and to, strangers, visitors, government employees, missionaries, R.C.M. and C.M.S., prospectors, miners, free trappers, and Indian hunters from the other posts or districts. One copy was retained at the outpost; the other enclosed with the outfit and accounts sent to the district manager. This was officially signed by the officer in charge and became a reliable legal document.

This book was officially called the *Journal of Daily Occurrences* (i.e. Diary). It was dated the first of June of current outfit (of each year). Correct list of post manager and engaged by: contract employees (married, single, or number of family); date and number of contract and salary of each; all births, marriages, or deaths with the exact dates. This was signed and witnessed. This book contained a reliable history of the country, as private information to the Hudson's Bay Company, and was, on occasion, the legal proof of births, marriages, deaths and successions, proof of wills, inheritance, etc., when no other legal proof could be obtained in the North-West Territories.

Herewith is a sample of a daily post journal:

District A. or R. (Athabaska or Mackenzie River District) Outfit—1863/4, or whatever year it might have been.

SAMPLE ONLY
JOURNAL OF DAILY OCCURRENCES

1st June 18? To 31st May 18?
(Say) Fort Resolution—R. Dist.—(Mackenzie River District)

Outfit 1863/4—June 1,—say Monday.
Day of the week—
Post manager's name.
Staff
Detailed—Engaged servants
" -Temporary—
" -Voyagers, boat or land.
Births, marriages, deaths, or any dismissals, deserters
Animals—Indian trading purposes.
Strangers of all kinds with or without receiving hospitality.
Weather fine light wind.
Receipts of fish for day from our fisherman.
No. ? 50 or 100.

Party of Indian Hunters
No. ? 20 with teams, etc. (If winter).
Fairly successful hunts—furs and meat.
Work—detailed—summer or winter—at post or on voyage.
Packets, etc.
Boats or sleds—arrived or departed—number of sleds or boats.
With P. L. L. Brigade (Distr. R) or Ft. Simpson
—Meat on fish boats or hay boats, etc.
Sickness—if any.
Prospects for increase of fur return or meat—etc.
Bills of lading of boats, sleds, etc.

Anything unusual or usual.
Sunday church service at 11 AM if three persons present.
Held by clerk or post manager, interpreter.
Sunday—no work. No Hudson Bay employee leaves the post by order on Sunday. Daily rations issued to man or dog about mid-day.

The story of Peers's ghost, famous throughout the country at this time, was seriously interfering with the fur trade. On March 15, 1853, Richard Augustus Peers, a fur trader in charge of Fort McPherson, Peel's river, died suddenly and was buried at the post. For the next seven years his ghost haunted the district.

Peers was an able officer, respected by the Company, and liked by the Indians. For eleven years he had been stationed at lonely northern posts where, he repeatedly said, he would not wish to be buried. Long before his death, he had made a will and hidden it in the trading shop, but Strachan Jones, who took temporary charge of the post, was unable to find it.

Peers's ghost, according to the story, appeared at the post at a certain time every night. The men heard a noise as of someone dragging chains and when they investigated they could find no cause for this noise. They decided that Peers was looking for his will. Jones's mind became so affected that he had to be transferred to Fort Rae. Peers's ghost followed him there. He had to be retired from the service.

From the time of Peers's death in 1853 until 1860, when his

body was finally buried at Fort Simpson, boatmen with the brigades that moored at Fort McPherson were bothered at night by the constant tapping of their boats. When they looked at them, the tapping ceased. When they withdrew, the tapping began again.

In the autumn of 1859, Peers's widow, then Mrs. Alexander McKenzie, urged Charles P. Gaudet, who was in charge of Fort McPherson, to convey the body of her former husband to Fort Simpson for burial. He arranged to take it by dog train to Fort Good Hope, a distance of three hundred miles, while Roderick MacFarlane, the officer at Fort Good Hope, undertook to deliver it at Fort Simpson, some five hundred miles further south. When exhumed, Peers's body was in perfect condition. There is constant frost at Fort McPherson, which is about one degree north of the Arctic Circle.

Mr. Gaudet arrived at Fort Good Hope on the first day of March 1860 and delivered Peers's body to Mr. MacFarlane. Here the coffin was fixed on a dog team and driven by Michael Thomas, an Iroquois Indian from Caughnawaga, Quebec. Mr. MacFarlane led the train, which carried blankets and provisions, on overshoes. After seven days, hard travelling through snow and ice the funeral train reached Fort Norman, two hundred miles on the last lap of the journey.

After a rest at this post, the driver of the baggage train from Fort Good Hope was exchanged for a new one, named Michel Iroquois, and fresh dogs were acquired. From here, Nicol Taylor, who had formerly served under Peers, volunteered to accompany the party and help beat the difficult track over snow and ice for the funeral cortege. Many times have I heard MacFarlane relate his experiences on this trip and give instances of Peers's ghostly presence.

Peers's ghost, he insisted, followed them all the way. At one time they distinctly heard Peers's voice command the dogs— *marché!* It was as if Peers's spirit were accompanying the party to make sure that his wishes in regard to his final burial would be carried out.

It is a fact that Peers's ghost affected many an officer of sound common sense and terrified the Indians. About the time Peers's body was buried at Fort Simpson, the trading store at

Fort McPherson was pulled down and Peers's will was discovered in a mortise in a beam. From that day, the ghost of Peel's river disappeared.

Gaudet (afterwards chief trader) was a man of great ability. At the time of Peers's death he was apprentice postmaster at La Pierre's House and during the summer of 1853 he was appointed to Fort McPherson, where he remained in charge until November, when Alexander McKenzie took over.

Gaudet married a daughter of Baptiste Hoole, the famous interpreter of the Yukon. He had several sons in the service of the Company.

One year during an epidemic of measles Gaudet was with the Red River brigade, commanded by Chief Factor William McMurray, taking his family out of the North. Between Cumberland and The Pas, two of his children died. He wanted the boats to return to Cumberland in order to bury his children, but the boatmen rebelled. Dr. William Aeneas MacKay, who was a passenger, persuaded Gaudet to bury the bodies temporarily on the banks of the river and to send a boat back to the fort with burial instructions.

The next day the boatmen demanded pay for the extra work of returning to the fort. There was an Irishman in the lot and a couple of English half-breeds. McMurray refused and the strikers left the boats, demanding provisions. "Rebel and starve!" McMurray told them. Things looked ugly. McMurray was extremely nice, but when defied he was a man to be reckoned with. When the men refused to work, he had all the provisions placed in his tent under guard. He instructed the guards to shoot the rebels if they attempted to touch it. The men built a raft and, without provisions and only a gun, started off down the river.

McMurray and Gaudet took the three boats, loaded to capacity, a hundred miles upstream with only a steersman and eight men of crew instead of the usual complement of eight men to a boat. They manned two of the boats with six men each, took them around two or three bends in the river, beached them, and returned for the third. In riding the rapids, McMurray and Gaudet each steered a boat, with four men to a boat on the tracking lines. They had to fight a strong current and a heavy wind. Three or four days' slow travelling got the brigade to The Pas. The rebels were sure McMurray couldn't go forward without them. The old-time Company officers and men were a special breed and seemed to be at their best when odds were against them. This was probably the first organized strike in the North-West.

CHAPTER 8

I Establish Fort Nelson

In the year 1864–65, I was at Fort Resolution when word came from Fort Garry that free traders were on their way to the Mackenzie River District. Upon investigation, we discovered that these free traders were entering the district by way of the Peace River, coming from Fort St. John to Fort Liard on the Liard River, which was a very rich beaver region. I was the only available clerk, so Mr. Hardisty decided to send me at once to Nelson River to establish a post. It would be my business to keep these traders from getting furs. Hardisty took me to Fort Simpson himself. Here he gave me reliable men—experienced fur men, boatmen, hunters—and good boats. I got to Nelson River about the end of September with my crew and outfit.

Among the men travelling with me were Collor Hoole, the famous interpreter of old Fort Yukon, Baptiste Forcier, and Francois Boileau. No ordinary boatmen, they were perhaps the finest in the service of the Company, which is saying much, for the Company had in its employ boatmen without peers. Also, I had two young Métis: Michael (I forgot his last name) and Baptiste Comptois; a fellow named Mackay, whose nickname was *la toupe*; Baptiste Forcier's son-in-law, a Métis, whom we called Simple Jack; and a Sikanni Indian. In addition to these men, I had to engage one or two others to complete my party to build Fort Nelson.

The choice of the site for the fort was left to my discretion. I decided to place it at a point where I could meet and watch the free traders who came into my territory. I travelled a hundred miles up Fort Nelson river to the point where, the Indians informed me, the traders coming from Peace River would strike it. The place looked suitable for a fort, so we set to work to build.

Like all our trading posts, our little establishment was modest. First we built a one-storey trading store, thirty by twenty feet, and a little house for me and my cook, Forcier, his fifteen-year-old step-son, and his little girl. Forcier's wife had died on the trip and we had buried her in a riverbank. Then we built a house for Francois Boileau, who had his wife and several children with him. The two single men had quarters with him. All houses were built of rough-hewn logs.

To maintain prestige, an officer of the Company had to have his own house and his personal servants. Hudson's Bay Company officers had great authority in the country. We were the administrators of law and order. We had authority to marry people, bury the dead, baptize—perform all the offices of the church and civil law.

Like other officers, I was thrown in with perhaps the hardest and roughest men in the territory of Canada and always we respected each other. The loyalty and obedience of the men to duty and to the commands of the Company were a tradition. I can think back over a span of more than seventy-five years to my days amongst them. I can forget much of their roughness and remember most of them kindly for their loyalty to me and to the Company. The prestige which we demanded may have something to do with it.

Early in November, when the Indians heard that I had come to establish a post, they came in from their hunting grounds, bringing their furs and great quantities of provisions. They had the furs of their previous winter hunt and also those of their spring hunt. They had all the meats of the region—moose, mountain goat, and sheep. We had sent word out by runners of our intention to establish a post, and the tribes had been collecting their furs in anticipation of our arrival. I had a great trade.

I had a list of the debts owed by the Indians at Fort Liard. After collecting them and paying the hunters for their provisions and furs, I gave them advances for the winter. One or two of the Indians, whom I engaged as fort hunters, stayed in the vicinity of the fort all winter. The rest of them—about twenty-five able, experienced hunters and their families and young men—went off for the winter to their hunting grounds.

I didn't expect to hear anything from these hunters until around Christmas, when it was customary for them to come back to the fort with their early catch of furs. Christmas arrived and not a word from them. I grew anxious. No hunters, no furs. Then one day a woman arrived in a half-starved condition to report that the whole band was down with sickness, that only she had escaped the disease. She said all were starving.

This was the year of the great scarlet fever epidemic, and it was the first I had heard of it. The disease had come into the Mackenzie River and to other parts of the country from Fort Garry. The epidemic swept through the whole Mackenzie River District. I lost half my Indians—the hunters with whom I had expected to trade.

I sent a party of men with provisions and instructions to bring the party to the fort. We had to do what we could to save their lives. They found more than half the party dead. We had only three sleds and on these they brought as many as they could of the sickest. All who could walk at all followed on foot. As soon as the sleds reached the fort, we unloaded the sick and sent the dog team back to the Indian camp, which was fifty miles from the fort. The weather was terribly cold. I had to send men out to bury those that had died on the trail. Out of the whole band, not more than fifteen of my good hunters were saved.

Presently, when the packet arrived from Fort Simpson via Fort Liard, I learned that the epidemic was bad and that the Indians were dying in numbers.

Although Fort Nelson[4] was built for the purpose of intercepting the free traders, it was never actually used for this purpose. When they heard that the epidemic had wiped out the hunters, they stayed away. The few Indians who were left were too feeble to hunt. I had to feed them and give them additional advances and take a chance on getting paid.

With things in this state, a band of Indians came from Devil's Lake on the south side of the mountains to hunt in the Beaver Indian country. They got quantities of furs, and my trade with these western Indians more than made up for my loss. The other districts hadn't such luck. I turned in a fine lot of business. The epidemic had successfully opposed the free traders.

Suddenly, Fort Nelson became an important post. Orders came from Fort Garry to place the most experienced clerk in the district in charge of it.

In the spring of 1865, I got word from Mr. Hardisty that Julian S. Onion[5] (Julian S. Camsell as he was known later), a senior clerk, would be sent to relieve me. By first open water in the spring, Camsell arrived. I handed the fort over to him and left for Fort Simpson. My party travelled in a couple of makeshift canoes as far as Fort Liard, where I got proper canoes to take me to Fort Simpson.

Fort Nelson still stands. The original building of course has been enlarged. It became in after years a great trading post. It remained undisturbed by free traders until the Klondike Gold Rush, when traders, miners, and prospectors came by way of Fort Saint John across to Fort Nelson, then up the Liard to the Yukon.

The guides of the boat brigade have gone, but their records remain. They were responsible men. It was well we realized it. When their boats pushed off from land, they alone were responsible for the lives of the crew and the cargoes of the Company. When the brigade arrived at the posts, the guides dined with the officer in charge. Their prestige was undisputed.

Their responsibility was heavy. If at bad rapids they hadn't complete confidence in the ability of the steersmen, they would run the boats themselves. This may sound unimportant to the layman, but to the Company it meant the safety of their valuable cargoes of furs, merchandise, or provisions.

The officials of the Company always had liquor. The guides took a glass with them and knew how to behave themselves. There was no drunkenness.

The officers were glad to have the guides take the responsibility of the boatmen. Even upon landing, the men took their orders from the guide, and they were responsible to him for their conduct while ashore. He was the chief authority. No officer of the

Company at any post concerned himself with the management of the men. These hardy voyageurs had to be handled with discretion. Take the dances—to speak plainly, the dances and amusements were provided to keep the men contented.

The guide, though a man of power, knew how to handle the men leniently as well as firmly. Always after a dance there were some who would not appear at his command. To these he paid no heed. He ordered the majority to the boats and got the brigade away. Not far distant from the post, he called a halt for a meal to give the laggards a chance to overtake the brigade. They always came.

Forcier's official position was Mackenzie River Guide and Winter Packeteer (West), that is, from Fort Simpson to Fort Liard to Fort Halkett. He held this appointment, Guide No. 2, for over forty years. He was born at St. Boniface and in his youth had been a summer trip man and plains hunter. He became such a skilful boatman that when a reliable guide was required for the Mackenzie River transport, he was dispatched to the post. I first met him and Joseph Bouvier, another noted guide, on my trip to Mackenzie's river in the summer of 1863.

Forcier was the perfect type of Métis, alert and intelligent. He knew his own mind and could meet any emergency. Like all the Red River men, he was a linguist. A perfect winter traveller, he could find his way anywhere in the North and under all circumstances. If his dog team played out, he unharnessed his dogs and pulled the sled himself. He never turned back from a trip.

Forcier had agreeable manners and was very sociable and good company, but he had a hard temper if enraged. His first wife was the daughter of Baptiste Le Noire (Black or Dusky Baptiste) and I think a Fort Simpson Indian woman. She died in 1864, as I have mentioned, on our trip between Fort Liard and Fort Nelson, leaving a daughter, named Rosalie, and a son by another marriage. Forcier's second wife was Scolastique Cadien, daughter of Baptiste Cadien, the celebrated interpreter. There were no children by this marriage. I regarded Forcier highly. He was respected in and out of the service. He died at Fort Chipewyan.

On our 1863 trip, Bouvier told me about the brigade he and Baptiste Bruce once took to Lewes and Pelly rivers. In passing Hell's Gate—this is the most dangerous river in the North—all the men except he and Bruce had been drowned. He said, "We lashed all oars to the boats and braced logs on the bottoms, inside. Bruce and I bound ourselves securely to our boats. The crew took the tracking lines and, from high on the rocks, fairly lifted our boats from the water. We did not use oars, just poles. We reached the main whirlpool. In their terrible fight to save us and the cargoes, all the men were hauled into the boiling rapids and drowned. Bruce and I got through. It was a terrible experience, but we were in our prime."

Chief Factor Campbell records this experience, which was about 1840. Upstream over this water it took the boats seven days with double crews to make the sixty-mile trip. It took seven hours to come down.

The breadth of the river at the narrowest point of this rapid is from 80 to 90 yards; at its widest about 150 to 200. I made a trip by land past this rapid on foot in the year 1865, on my way to Fort Halkett, where I journeyed to interview the clerk about debts which the Sikanni Indians owed my post and his. Fort Halkett, built after the union of 1821 and abandoned in 1875, was at the junction of the Liard and Smith rivers and was a highway to the west.

Bouvier, like Forcier, had advanced from boatman and steersman for the Company on the Red River to become a guide for the Mackenzie River brigade of three boats, crew of ten. It would be impossible to make anyone unacquainted with the North understand the importance of the work of these northern guides. They had to take their boats across Great Slave Lake, about two hundred miles, then over Lake Athabaska, and make ten portages between Slave Lake and the height of land at Portage La Loche, each from ten to twelve miles. The Portage La Loche ran from Clearwater River to Buffalo River. In dangerous situations Bouvier and Forcier would run all three boats themselves.

I listened to many strange tales on my way to Mackenzie's river.

Bouvier and Forcier told me about the terrible tragedy at Fort Halkett. Peter P. was in charge. He was from Edmonton District and under Chief Factor William Christie. Anyway, it was around 1848 that Peter P., faced with starvation, had eaten his two men, Forbister and Debois. Bouvier and Forcier were the men who discovered Peter starving. The story was known to every one in Mackenzie's river. I record the story as I remember it from

Bouvier. These guides were important and reliable men. They came under my command. Bouvier said:

> Forcier and I were taking the Hudson's Bay winter packet to Campbell at the forks of the Lewes and Pelly. We were on foot, hauling our small supplies on a sled. We hadn't any dog team in those days. We got near the Fort Halkett post. We saw no smoke from the chimney. A little closer we came. The parchment windows were gone. Now in the North this is a sign of starvation. Inside we found Peter. He was like a skeleton. He sat over a little spark of fire, hardly able to move. We asked about the men who were stationed with him. He could hardly speak, but he made out to us that they had gone to hunt and had not come back. Forcier scraped the ashes back from the little fire to get a coal for his pipe. There were human bones. We decided that Peter had eaten his men. We fixed him up with more food than we could spare and cleared out as fast as God would let us.
>
> It was a bad winter. No game had come to the post. All the Indians were starving. We left almost all our small provisions with Peter. We had nothing for ourselves, except what we managed to kill on the way. Before we got to Campbell's post, we had to boil and eat Forcier's extra pair of leather (Company) trousers. They had bone buttons. The leather was tough. A button stuck in Forcier's throat and almost choked him. After we left Peter, a Sikanni Indian called at his post with meat. Word got to the Liard post about Peter's condition and provisions were sent as fast as possible.

Often on this trip to Mackenzie's river both Forcier and Bouvier joked about the time they had eaten boiled trousers and bone buttons. Peter, when rescued, was a fearful sight. The men who got to his relief found the clothes, hair, and bones of the missing men buried near the post under roots of trees. Enquiries were not pressed. The thing was too serious. The chief factors and other officers of the Company in the country had to use their best judgment in affairs of this sort. None knew better than they the hardships that men placed beyond civilization had to face. What was the use of hanging the poor fellow?

Word of the tragedy got about amongst the Indians and nothing on earth would induce them to go near Peter's post. There was a superstition in the country that once a man had eaten human flesh he had a taste for it. Peter was taken, or retired, out of the service. He lived near the Roman Catholic mission of Lac Là Biche. I saw him there on my travels from post to post from 1863 on. He was a miserable kind of fellow and a horrible disfigured sight. He had eaten his lips away, and his teeth and gums lay exposed. He died at Lac Là Biche.

It is possible that Peter is the "Mr. P" mentioned in Campbell's journal. I have read this journal. He gives Frances Lake, an outpost or flying post of Fort Halkett—sixty or seventy miles away—as the place where Peter was stationed. I suppose he naturally felt it a matter of policy to avoid mentioning Peter's name and Fort Halkett as the place where this act of cannibalism took place.

Forcier was a great trapper and, between his boat trips, he used to trap in a considerable way. One day he brought home a young live fox that he had found in one of his traps. His wife was sitting by the chimney. He threw the fox into her lap—playfully. When her child was born it had a head shaped like a fox and it cried like an animal. The body was normal. The mother was terrified and considered the child a devil. They were advised to kill the child instantly because an abnormal child like this would have created fear amongst the tribes and anger at white men. Forcier stuffed moss into the child's mouth—choked it painlessly to death. The affair was kept quiet. Forcier told me this story himself. He was with me in 1864 when I built Fort Nelson. This sad affair had happened about fifteen years before I met him. Forcier was a reliable man not only in the boats but in every class of work. The death of this abnormal child seemed to be on his mind.

From the summer of 1863, when I first met Joseph Bouvier, until 1884, I travelled with him almost continuously during the summer boating seasons. He was a well-developed, healthy man, at least six feet tall. One saw at a glance that he was no ordinary man. He gave his orders in French, English, Slavey, Montagnais, Chipewyan—in the language which was handiest. He, too, was a trusted packeteer, carrying the winter mails for the Company. He married a daughter of Francois Beaulieu and he had a large family. He died, brave fellow, on a trip on Great

Slave Lake in the vicinity of Fort Resolution. There is a pathetic story connected with his unexpected death. I respected and admired Bouvier greatly.

Francois Beaulieu was of French and Iroquois extraction and was a character of importance on Mackenzie's river. He and another patriot, Jean Alexandre, had fled north from Quebec after the Papineau Rebellion into Hudson's Bay territory, where only the law of the Company held. They settled at the salt springs near Fort Smith in the Athabaska District. These fellows became small traders for the Company.

From the salt springs on the Salt River, we got the salt we required for our posts. Beaulieu very wisely secured a grant of land from the Company beside the springs in return for supplying salt for the brigades. He had great influence with the Indians and Chief Factor William McMurray, who was in charge of the district, considered it good policy to retain his friendship.

Beaulieu soon established a settlement around the salt springs, and for more than fifty years he, assisted by Alexandre, terrorized the natives as far north as Fort Liard. On one occasion the pair attacked a band of Great Bear Indians, seized the women, and killed all the other members of the band.

Once W. L. Hardisty was taking a brigade up the river to Portage La Loche when, near Beaulieu's place on Salt River, the boat crew, who were Mackenzie River Indians, rebelled. Hardisty sent for Beaulieu. The old dictator came, pulled out his long knife, and pretended to shave his tobacco plug. "Get back to your boats and give no more trouble to your chief!" he told the rebels, who took to their boats. They feared Beaulieu's knife. Hardisty gave the old rascal a suitable present for his trouble.

As leading man amongst the Fort Rae Indians, the Company granted Beaulieu a yearly gratuity and other privileges and courtesies, as he was a great asset to our fur trade. He took advantage of his prestige by keeping his account heavily overdrawn and by constantly demanding goods that we did not carry. The clerks at the Fort Rae post stood in awe of him.

In 1866 when I returned to Fort Rae, Beaulieu arrived and instructed me to order a hand sewing machine and a music box for him. I advised him firmly that he was already in considerable debt to the Company and that I would not only not order the sewing machine and the music box, but would not extend further credit to him until he had brought furs to settle his debt. "I'll go to Fort Simpson and have Mr. Camsell (district officer) send a clerk to Fort Rae who will suit me," he said, and cleared out.

He took several dog sleds of fresh caribou meat (as a peace offering, but really to sell) to Camsell and reported me in Dogrib, *"Nazular, nazular, e-stushy, nazular!"* This meant that I was no good, never had been any good, and never would be better.

Camsell and I often laughed over this doubtful compliment. Camsell enjoyed Beaulieu's visit, took his meat on account, spoke firmly about his overdrawn account, and gave him a little clever sympathy. Beaulieu came back ready to overlook the incident of the sewing machine. The old fellow ended his stormy life on the Salt River.

The original Fort Rae[6], or Fort Providence as it was then called, was established by Alexander Mackenzie for the North West Company in 1790 on Great Slave Lake at the mouth of Yellowknife River. In 1852, the Hudson's Bay Company moved the post to an island on the north arm of the lake and renamed it Fort Rae, after Dr. John Rae, who spent some time there and put up a few buildings as a base for his supplies. Later the fort was partly removed and built at the end of Willow River, ten miles distant, but it was finally returned to its present position.

This post was generally called Mountain Island fort as it was built originally on an island but with the diversion of water it became a peninsula. The natives who came to trade always called it Mountain Island fort and they could not be induced to call it Fort Rae. Dr. Rae had found the position suitable for transportation. The old log buildings which he put up were improved and added to by Chief Factor Roderick MacFarlane and by Laurence Clarke. I built several additional houses at the post at various times between 1864 and 1875 when I was stationed there. In my day, this post was a very important provision post and one of the few posts where we got muskoxen.

Dr. Rae and his second wife, Miss Catherine Thompson, were my great friends. The last time I dined with them was when I was in England in 1875. They were living in Lexholm Gardens, West Kensington. Dr. Rae was a fine looking man. He was a great marksman, walker, and traveler. He was a graduate of Edinburgh University and this university gave him an honorary LL.D.; McGill University gave him an honorary M.D.

There are some peculiar geological formations at Fort Rae. Opposite the fort on the mainland, there is an underground river which empties into the lake. It runs from five or six miles back under the hills. From these hills, we used to drop stones through crevices in the rocks. We could count twenty before we heard them splash into the river below. There is a sandy beach where this little underground river empties into Great Slave Lake, and always in the sand there were peculiar marks (tracks of birds or animals, no doubt, or patterns formed by the winds) which the Indians regarded as footprints of Indian spirits returned down this mysterious river to dance. They regarded this river with great awe. And for another reason: the underground river was full of small fish—like minnows, but without eyes. Neither I nor my men could discover eyes in these funny little fish.

CHAPTER 9

I Walk Across
the Barren Lands

In 1867 when I was in charge of Fort Rae, I went on a trading and exploratory trip from there to Fort Norman by way of Great Bear Lake. I was anxious to get a record from Nicol Taylor, the post manager, of his accounts with the Dogrib hunters so that I would know how much credit I could safely let them have when they came to Fort Rae to trade. I camped on the site of the present Giant Yellowknife gold mines. As no one but Indians had ever made that trip, I was the first white man to do so.

I made careful arrangements for the journey and started with four dogsleds, provisions, some trading goods, two Indian guides, and my general servant, Louis La Ferte, the renowned interpreter and traveller.

In my own team, I had four strapping dogs. Their mother ran loose. Sometimes I harnessed her to give the others, in turn, freedom. La Ferte, my man, had five dogs also; the other men had the same complement. We never rode on our sleds—we ran ahead, walked beside, or followed.

As we, the officers of the Company, were first, last, and always traders with the interest of the Company at heart, I decided to

take the out-of-the-way but well-beaten trail to Marten Lake to
visit Beaulieu, the chief of the camps, who had about thirty capable hunters. He was the son of the famous Beaulieu who fled into
the North after the Papineau Rebellion. Marten Lake was a fine
wintering place for caribou, and Beaulieu had a good fishing base.
We spent a day at this camp, trading and arranging with a party of
his Indians to take our furs, meat, and stuff back to Fort Rae.

When we got off, heading easterly for Bear Lake, I noticed that
the nature of the country began to alter. When we left the Strong
Woods to go on to the Barren Lands, we saw great herds of
deer—thousands and thousands—on their way to winter in the
Strong Woods Mountains. The whole country was such a net-
work of deer tracks that we could hardly find foot space between
them. I had difficulty in keeping my hunters from shooting them.
I didn't want to be burdened with meat or skins, but on the second day from Beaulieu's camp, I let them shoot a deer and eat all
they wanted. I will say this for my men, much as they wanted to
hunt, there was no insubordination. I was both an officer and the
Hudson's Bay Company, and recognized as such.

The third day found us travelling through trees though we
were north of the timberline and approaching the Barren Lands.
Another day's travel took us out of trees and into shrubs. During
the next two days the country changed again. There was nothing
to be seen but rocks and small shrubs. We passed several large
lakes about two or three miles long and one-half mile wide. The
deer tracks had now almost completely disappeared.

On the fifth day from Beaulieu's camp, I noticed two hills in
the distance. By the compass, we were heading more northeast
than in a direct line to Great Bear Lake. Indians are sensitive. I did
not ask questions. It was wise for an officer not to appear too
ignorant about the country.

On the sixth day, I understood why my guides had taken this
out-of-the-way route. We came to a long narrow lake, from fifteen
to twenty miles long and varying in width from a half to a mile,
that led directly between the hills and was separated by two narrows. At one of the narrows there was a large wooden cross
made out of timber, which must have been brought on sleds
from the timber region—men could not have carried it that far.
My man, La Ferte, said it marked the point to which Père Petitot

had come some years before. This cross stood approximately mid-way between Great Slave and Great Bear lakes. Père Petitot's book, now out of print, will confirm what I say. (There is a copy of it in the Archives of St. Boniface.) Père Petitot was a clever man. The last time I talked to Bear Lake people, the cross still stood.

Leaving the end of this lake, we crossed a plateau three or four miles in length which, the guides said, overlaid a huge salt bed. The ground was bare of snow and the salt affected the dogs' feet, making them lame. We had to put dog shoes on them. The ground was greyish white in colour and had a salty taste. It was hard hauling—much like going over frozen sand. We crossed this salt plain as quickly as we could, heading directly for the two hills and into the long valley which held the lake.

Soon the country became rolling and rocky and for a couple of days the general appearance of the scenery remained the same. We met more timber wolves than on the first part of our trip—travelling in little bands of seven or eight—on their way from the coast, following the deer to the Horn Mountains. Their scent excited our dogs and we could hardly keep them from giving chase. Northern dogs were ferocious and anything they saw they wanted to kill. Our best sled dogs were a crossbreed—civilized dogs crossed with huskies. They were fine dependable dogs to us, their masters, but savage to strangers.

I wore sensible and suitable clothes. We did not go in for spectacular dress. I had a deerskin capote, buckskin coat, blue stroud leggings with little red stripes down the sides (we permitted ourselves this bit of ornamentation, as we carried these leggings in stock), moose-skin moccasins, duffle socks, with a thin pair of worsted socks next my feet, and moose-skin mitts. For sleeping, each man carried a caribou skin robe, a three-point Hudson's Bay blanket, and a canvas sheet six to eight feet long and a yard wide to spread on the ground. At night, we rolled ourselves first in the blanket, then in the robe. We had no shelter of any kind against the weather, except what we could get from placing our sleds on edge to form a snow or wind break.

We were able to gather enough twigs during the day to boil our kettle at night. We melted snow for cooking and drinking water. La Ferte and I had pemmican and bannock. The Indians had fresh meat, which they cut thick and ate raw. Sometimes they scorched it a little over the fire when we boiled the kettle.

In the valleys I noticed great bands of ptarmigan. The flocks rose in thousands. In summer these birds live on lichens and kinnikinic berries, which are berries like cranberries; in the winter they eat frozen berries, which remain on the bushes and are plentiful.

The Barren Lands are vast and rolling and covered with rocks. There is no subsoil. It was a new world to me after the great rivers of Mackenzie's river basin.

As we drew close to Bear Lake, we could see from high ground what I thought was a mirage. This was Bear Lake. It seemed near, but in the clear atmosphere the distance was deceiving. Instead of striking it, as I thought we would, in half a day, it took us the best part of two. On the border of the lake we found small timber in the valleys and in the cracks of the rocks. Some of it was six or seven inches in diameter at the stump.

We struck the lake at a place which my guides called Bear Point, and here we made camp. Nearby was a great cave, my guides said. I asked them to take me to it, but they were unwilling. I said I would go.

This great cave, which ran into the hill for fifty or sixty yards, was a cavity left by a rock the size of a large house which had slipped away from the main rock into the water. It looked from a distance like a great bear's head, so the lake had been named by the Indians. I went into the cave and there found bones of birds, fish, and animals. I was surprised to find great quantities of arrows to which bits of coloured calico were attached. My guides were nervous. They told me, hesitatingly, that the cave was inhabited by the *mucha* (bad) *Manitou* and that Indians never visited it but satisfied the evil Manitou by firing decorated arrows into it as they went past in their canoes. This cave is shown on Franklin's map of his 1825-26 discoveries as "Cave and Isles of the Manito."

From Bear Point my guides took me straight across the lake to the site of old Fort Franklin, which was built by Sir John Franklin's party. Only the ruins of the old post stood. I made out the fallen walls of houses which had been built of stone and the remains of chimneys about four or five feet high. It seemed strange to see a sundial standing near the ruins. Fort Franklin was about fifty miles—a full day's travel on the ice—from Bear Point and about sixty miles from Fort Norman.

I was three days at the post getting my business arranged, exchanging lists of Indian debts with Taylor, and visiting with Mr. Bompas, the missionary. Bompas said, "I am expecting letters, in connection with the diocese, by the spring packet. By writing to Fort Simpson, my answers will be delayed for a year. Let me go with you as far as Fort Rae. From there I can get to Fort Resolution, meet the packet, and examine and answer my letters."

"Much as I dislike to," I said, "I shall have to refuse your request. It would be folly for you to come. It has taken experienced men twenty-one days, fast travelling, to walk the 450 miles between the posts." I couldn't discourage him. He kept pleading with me to take him. "God will take care of us!" he said. I raised all kinds of objections, but I couldn't put him off. Finally, the next morning I agreed to let him accompany us. "It is a matter of life and death," I told him, "and you will have to assume the risk of starvation and exposure." I made him sign a written agreement freeing me of responsibility.

We got off at dawn the next morning. It was a fine bright day and the sky was lightened by flashing northern lights. But it was cold! I learned afterwards that the thermometer at Fort Norman that night had registered 70 degrees below, the then lowest known record at this post. It was the only time in the country that I knew the mercury to go as low as that.

Great Bear Lake is a wonderful lake. You can see through the thick, clear ice to the bottom. Bompas had a little bedding—mighty little—a small bag of provisions, and a box of chocolates. His provision bag weighed 10 pounds. I had warned him to travel light, as my dogs could not be burdened with extra baggage. He had, altogether, 50 pounds of dunnage. Altogether, my dogs had a load of 250 pounds, which was light enough for fast travelling.

My man, La Ferte, carried about 250 pounds of general provisions on his sled and some fish for his dogs. Bompas was a passenger against my will. La Ferte and the Indian guides had objected, as much as they dared, to Bompas coming with us. Before we had got two hundred yards, the cold and intense wind, which was three-quarters behind us, sent us at a run over the ice. My dogs went at a smart rate, five or six miles an hour. This was nothing for them or for me.

But what about Mr. Bompas? He was a good walker, but six

miles an hour was too much for him. He fell behind. On ahead the guides and La Ferte were moving fast. I followed them, losing a little. Presently I began losing sight of Bompas. Even if I called, my men were too far ahead to hear. I could not leave my minister in order to overtake them. He might get lost or frozen. I realized suddenly what I was up against. What I had feared was happening. The man *couldn't* travel! With great difficulty, I managed to stop my dogs. It was bitterly cold and they were moving fast to keep warm. Finally Bompas caught up, numb. I got him on the sled. "I must catch up to my men," I said. "Unless you travel faster, you'll freeze!"

It isn't easy to sit on a loaded sleigh, swaying as the dogs trot. Bompas kept bouncing off. After he had fallen off half a dozen times, I stopped my dogs. We were now far behind my men. The only thing I could do was to tie Bompas to the sled. I got a tail line around his body and fastened him on top of the load. This took time. My men, still travelling fast, were now a couple of miles ahead, lost to sight. On the smooth ice, they had left no trail. Bompas was freezing, he was utterly helpless, but I couldn't pay any attention to him. I hurried after my men. After a while I discovered that Bompas was getting loose. I stopped, wrapped my blanket robe around him, tied him fast to the load again, and drove my dogs on at top speed. And I *could* travel in those days!

But now I was uncertain about my direction. About five o'clock that afternoon I got across the ice and made for the point where my men should be. There was no sign of them. I said to Bompas, "Go to the woods, get something for a fire, and boil the kettle. I'll go a couple of miles along this side of the point. By that time you'll have the fire and be warm." I ran most of the way. Not a sign of my men nor of their having made camp. Not a track did I see. I came back to Bompas, who had only a little spark of fire. Down the other side of the point I went back. No sign! Bompas hadn't improved his fire. I got wood and boiled the kettle. After a bit of supper, I fed the dogs, made a sort of camp, and we rolled up in our blankets for the night. It is a wonder Bompas didn't freeze. He hadn't enough covering to keep him warm. Most of the night he was doubled up with cramps.

We had a cup of tea in the morning. Then I told Bompas that it was a case of life or death for us both, separated as we were from my men. I said I intended taking him back to Fort Norman. He pleaded with me so urgently to continue the trip that I gave in. Thinking I would overtake my men, I went on. I had no track to guide me. I knew only the general direction. We didn't bother much about compasses in the North. The North Star, the winds, and common instinct were our guides. There wasn't much snow. The travelling was all right for the dogs, but I was alone with a green traveller, practically without food, and hundreds of miles from Fort Rae.

I drove on. As on the previous day, Bompas kept falling behind, delaying me. I had to wait until he rubbed the cramps out of his legs. Finally, I had to put him on the sled again. I was walking at the rate of five or six miles an hour. At places where deer had passed, the scent excited the dogs and they wanted to go off on a chase. This caused delay. The only way I could control them was to stop and tie a line from my lead dog to my belt. I didn't tie Bompas very tight and he kept falling off, then I lost time tying him on again.

We got over the day. Now we were in the barren region. I kept on the lookout for twigs. I picked up every one I saw and put it in the breast of my jacket for a fire at night. I didn't stop during the day to make a fire. My provisions were on La Ferte's sled. I kept expecting to overtake him. Meanwhile Bompas's box of chocolates saved us from starvation.

This kind of travelling went on for four or five days. I had given up all hope of overtaking my men and I was no longer sure of my direction. The dogs were pretty tired at night from hauling Bompas. I generally set them free when we made camp. They would chase deer or wolves during the day, but at night they would not leave me. I had brought them up and they were faithful.

On the fifth day from Fort Norman I began watching for the two hills we had come between on our outward journey, in order to get on the track of my men. It was on the sixth day that I saw the hills in the distance. I reached them with all speed and went down the valley, looking for the long lake. There it lay! Now I would find tracks!

When I got to the south end of the lake, I made out in the distance some black objects which, when I reached them, proved to be poles set in the ice by Indian fishermen to hold their nets.

The Indians ought to be nearby. I followed their tracks to the woods only to find they had moved their tents. I picked up their tracks again and walked six miles before I found their camp. My men, they said, had camped at the lake the day before and gone on. I made up my mind that I would overtake them.

I tried to get the Indians to go back after Bompas. They refused. He was a Protestant; they were Roman Catholic. I had to go back for him myself. I got some meat and stuff from the Indians for my passenger and myself and for my dogs. My worry was over. I felt better tempered. My dogs—my leader—would not lose the track of the other dogs once they had found it. I think they had followed the scent of the dogs over the clear ice and all the way. They were highly intelligent.

As I travelled, I was struck by the faithfulness of my dogs. They seemed to realize the great danger we were in and were trying to catch up with our party. Always they pushed on, never wanting me to go ahead to lead them. In my heart, I depended on them to get me back to the fort. Now when Bompas fell off the sled, I was more pleasant about tying him on. Still, I was afraid he would die before I got him to the fort. He had bad cramps and was really sick.

We followed my men for five days. I was gaining on them and I made up my mind not to overtake them, but to keep half a day's travel behind. We were almost out of grub. My load was considerably lighter. My dogs had eaten almost all their provisions. How they could travel! They were on the tracks of their mates, and it was all I could do to hold them back in their eagerness to reach the fort. For the first time on that long, nervous trip I sat on the sled and took it easy. Bompas weighed about 160 pounds, I about 150. Our combined weights restrained the dogs a little.

My minister had a miserable time that trip, but he never grumbled. I shall never forget his reply when he kept falling off the sled and I, tired and worried, said, "What kind of legs have you got that you can't hang on?" It was, "Mr. King, the Lord 'taketh not pleasure in the legs of a man,' Psalm 147, verse 10." I said, "Well, what the devil did he give us legs for?" My plight was too desperate to listen to preachments. Bompas didn't continue the topic. A good fellow, Bompas, afterwards Bishop Bompas. If the trip was hard for me, it was harder for him. He did all he could to help.

After three or four days' more travelling, we struck the tip of the north arm of Great Slave Lake, about twenty-four miles from Fort Rae. Judging from one of their fireplaces to another it was easy to figure that I was only half a day behind my men.

When we approached Willow River late one day, I knew by the trail marks that my men would camp in a certain place. I decided to camp a few miles behind. I placed my camp in a position to disguise the smoke of my fire and where my dogs would be thrown off the scent of the other dogs. We had almost no food—just a scrap a day.

Being so close to the fort, they would not, I knew, start out very early in the morning. I arranged my own start accordingly. It was my first leisure on that harassing trip. We ate the scraps of food. Our sled was light and I could hardly check my excited dogs. An hour's travelling brought us to where the men had camped; there was still a fire burning. We stopped and made some tea. Then we took to the ice. I could make out specks in the distance. They were my men. I was travelling faster than they were. I jumped onto my sleigh and let my dogs have their way. When my men left the lake for the trail that led to the fort, I raced after them. On ahead, as I drove up, I saw La Ferte stop to talk to the men at the store door, then go off.

I drove to the store and asked my assistant, John Hope, what report La Ferte had given about my absence. La Ferte had said that after waiting a day for me at Bear Lake he concluded that I had taken Bompas back to Fort Norman and that I would return by way of Fort Simpson. The Indians came, shook hands, and made a great fuss over me. They were amazed to hear that I had made the trip alone, almost without food, and in such a short time.

It took me some time to forgive La Ferte. He was a good servant. I may be wrong, but I still feel that religion was at the bottom of the thing. After this, La Ferte had a great respect for me as a traveller. It took us twenty-one days to get to Fort Norman. It took us only seventeen to return.

I sent two packeteers, two men, and sufficient supplies with Bompas to meet the packet at Fort Resolution. I gave them my dogs. They were the best at the post.[7] He met the Fort Garry packet and was able to attend to the business for which he had come at such peril. He took the packet to Fort Simpson and was safely off my hands.

Some years later, Bompas had a narrow escape from death amongst the Eskimo. He went with an Indian, who had come to the fort to trade, over Peel's river, a distance of two hundred miles from the fort. Soon after his arrival some accidents befell members of the tribe and others got sick. The Eskimo blamed Bompas.

They decided to kill him, but the chief, who had considerable respect for Company men, ordered Bompas to leave at once. Bompas refused to believe that his life was in danger, but the chief put him on a sled and sent him, with two trusted men, back to the fort. The date was between 1867 and 1870.

CHAPTER 10

I Trade with the Loucheux Hunters

C ollor Hoole, the famous Métis interpreter of old Fort Yukon, who had accompanied my brigade of three boats, men, and provisions from Fort Resolution to establish Fort Nelson, gave me a great deal of first-hand information about the country and the Loucheux Indians who inhabited it.

The old interpreter was at this time over eighty years of age, but was well preserved and still capable and active. From Fort Simpson to Fort Liard he talked most of the time. His yarns were absorbing. In his young days he had been a great hunter for the Company at old Fort Yukon.

I discussed the folklore of the country also with Hoole's son, Antoine Hoole, who had been born and brought up at old Fort Yukon, and with the Loucheux themselves with whom I traded later at Fort Good Hope and Bear Lake. I learned much too from the Reverend Macdonald, who was an authority on the Loucheux people.

The original Loucheux tribe, according to legend, had been driven from Asia by another and stronger nation. They eventually found themselves on the shores of the Arctic Ocean, where the tribe became separated. One party reached the Yukon, where, finding the country full of game—moose, bear, beaver, fish—they settled and became numerous. The other division was lost. This legend was so fixed in the minds of the Loucheux that in my time they would ask every strange white man they met if he had at any time come across the other division of their people. The Loucheux were divided into two sections: the Capot Rouge (Red Coat) and Jimmy's Band.

To my mind the Loucheux are the most intelligent of the northern tribes. I was not long at the northern posts before discovering that in some respects the laws of the Loucheux Indians are similar to our own British laws. Their whole system of tribal government differs completely from those of other tribes in Mackenzie's river as do their methods of hunting.

A chieftainship descends by male line as long as it exists. Lacking male issue, the title descends to the next of kin in the female line, providing this female is the mother of seven sons. Andrew Fleet's wife was chieftess of the Loucheux tribe. Andrew Fleet was clerk in charge of the post at Peel's river and La Pierre's House. Educated at the mission school, Mrs. Fleet became expert in speaking and translating English into her own tongue. She helped Mr. Macdonald (afterwards archbishop), the minister in charge of that district, translate the scriptures into Loucheux. Mr. Macdonald's wife was also a Loucheux chieftess.

The Loucheux are fire worshippers. Their legends about creation are similar to those in the Bible. Their marriage customs are by elopement or purchase. If the latter, the prospective father-in-law is given a fee, a horse or its equivalent value, a dog, or a bundle of furs for the girl. In christening, a string is tied around the child's waist and the child is thrown into the river or lake. Often the shock kills the child. Children inherit the mother's name.

Death amongst the old people is voluntary. Those who become blind, crippled, helpless, or a burden to their people ask the younger members of the tribe to form into a party and provide a feast. This feast sometimes extends through several evenings until the old person has told the story of his life for the sacred preservation in the traditions of the family and the tribe. At the conclusion of the history, the old person is handed a noose to place around his neck. After giving final instructions about the disposition of his body, he hands the end of the rope to his closest relative, usually his son. The son receives the rope, places his feet against his father's back, and pulls gently. The noose tightens, the old person chokes, and all is over.

The body is kept for an hour or two amongst the mourners then prepared for burial according to the wishes of the deceased. If it is to be burned, a fire is prepared, reverently. A half dozen green poles are cut and laid in line. Small dry wood is spread on top of this, the body laid carefully upon it, and a fire lit. Two men, one on each side of the fire, attend to the cremation. The cremation is conducted with great feeling and ceremony.

I, who have lived long amongst the tribes and have witnessed and experienced the treachery and cruelty of the North, consider this a sensible and merciful way of ending a suffering life. It is impossible for Indians who are constantly travelling to carry their old and sick. It is agony, too, for old, feeble, and sick people to be jostled about, cold and hungry and in all kinds of weather.

The Loucheux hunting territory extends from some two hundred miles east of the Yukon River to the coast. It is not a large hunting territory, but it is a rich one. The Yukon River runs into the Pacific at Fort St. Michaels, close to Bering Strait. This river has three main tributaries—the Porcupine River, the Lewes River, and the Pelly River. Moose, Strong Wood deer, and caribou in the migrating season—most kinds of animals except badger and skunk—are native to the region.

One Loucheux method of trapping deer is similar to that once practised by the Plains Indians to catch buffalo. Deer are shy and even the most unsuspicious hillocks or clumps of moss will frighten them. In timbered areas, the hunters set up barriers of trees which extend out four or five miles from the wide wings of a corral. Into these barriers they direct the deer and drive them into the corrals, which are about an acre in area and protected by strong fences reinforced inside by pointed poles. In open country they make fences of moss and direct the animals into natural corrals or drive them over precipices. In my day, slaughter was on a wholesale scale. The hunters used bows and arrows and were so skilful that they could kill an animal with a single arrow.

The Loucheux were clever too at catching deer in snares. The snares were made of eight-foot strips of plaited rawhide (babiche) the thickness of a man's little finger. At one end, a double noose or buckle large enough to admit the head of a deer, antlers and all, was fixed. The other end also had a small noose. The hunters placed these snares on the deer runways. One end of the snare was tied to a long pole, which was placed at an angle in the ground. The noose, or buckle, was tied with strong grasses to willows or trees on each side of the deer run. When the deer got his head into the noose and started to run, the pole dragged, the noose gradually tightened, and the animal choked; also the pole dragged and caught in the trees. Tied properly, the noose could not slacken.

This was a simple and easy method of catching deer. The skin was unharmed, there was no cost for ammunition, little time lost, and the snares were working day and night. We encouraged the Indians in this method of trapping. Women followed the snares, skinning and dressing the animals.

The hunters used rawhide to construct and grass to fasten their snares, so as to eliminate man scents which deer could easily detect. They were careful to keep the odour of tobacco off their hands and the snares away from their clothes. Even rabbits could scent tobacco and dirty hands.

The Loucheux skinned the whole animal—head, feet, tail. We paid a high price for these skins, as there was a demand in England for skins dressed in this fashion. We tried, unsuccessfully, to get the tribes at other posts to dress their furs in the Loucheux style. Skins dressed in this way were clumsy and cost more to pack over land and water, but this was of no consideration when the Company was eager to meet the demands of the London market.

In all my experiences with furs, I never found anyone who could compare with the Loucheux women in dressing skins. They dressed moose skins the same as deer, very soft. This was unusual.

In the North, rabbit skins were made into robes. We traded in rabbit-skin robes only. For a good rabbit-skin robe—the size of a four-point blanket—we paid ten made beaver. It took about two hundred skins to make a robe of this size.

To make a robe, the green skins were first cut into strips—an inch and a half wide—round and round or up and down the skin in order to make each strip as long as possible. Each strip measured from eight to ten feet. These strips were wound on a reel, which was shaped like a bow and attached to a long handle, one end being fastened securely to the end of the bow. The women would take the handle of this bow, or reel, and twirl it round and round until the green skins were twisted into a strong rope. The twisted skins were then plaited over a frame, the exact size of a trade blanket, into a robe.

As a rule we had the women encase these robes in calico or print. They made excellent bed coverings for use at the posts as they were lighter than blankets and warmer. These light warm robes were extremely valuable to hunters. When I first went into the North, the Indian hunters used rabbit-skin robes entirely. Later, they demanded trade blankets.

In trapping bears, the Loucheux preferred their primitive methods. They set a thick log between two stout trees, attaching bait to it. The opening to the deadfall was about three feet. When the bear attacked the bait, pulling the string, the cleverly laid log fell and held him fast. There was no damage to the fur.

We sold some iron traps to the Indians, but not many. Traps weighed from six to eight pounds each, so freighting them on men's backs made them expensive. Each one cost the Indians from twenty to thirty made beaver, about one pound, or five dollars. We handled only smooth traps, as those with teeth damaged the furs.

Wolverines could elude the most persistent trappers. They used to dig underneath a bear trap and take the bait without springing it. A lone wolverine often starved out a whole camp of Indians by springing and robbing their traps and hauling their nets out of water. When a wolverine got on the trail of a trapper, he might as well clear out.

A wolverine would take a trap set for him, which was always set upside down on account of this propensity for burrowing, spring it, and carry it away. It was an everyday occurrence for a wolverine to find and rob the cache of a hunter even when it was placed on a high scaffold.

The Loucheux hunters devised a clever way of protecting fish (dog feed) from wolverines. They inserted a pole in the ice and to it tied their bags of fish and a few bells. The bells scared the wolverines. Another method was to dig a hole in the ice, put their fish into it, fill the hole with water, and let it freeze over. Wolverines could not dig through ice. In summer the hunters could always catch fish for their dogs. The Loucheux said that wolverines were evil Indians returned to earth in this form. After observing the craft of these animals and listening to Indian tales about them, we almost agreed with the Indian superstition.

Hunting birds with bows and arrows was one of the great pastimes of the Loucheux, who were expert marksmen. Even the children were skilful with their arrows. For serious hunting of game birds, they chose arrows in preference to guns. They also caught birds by line swinging. To the ends of long lines of twisted sinew, about twenty or thirty fathoms, they tied three or four lines and attached stones to the ends. In swinging these lines in different ways their arms formed nooses and caught the flying birds. The Loucheux were expert at line swinging and snared ducks, geese, swans, and many other varieties of birds in this fancy way of hunting. The only birds that wintered in the Loucheux region were ptarmigan, ravens, and owls, but there were many kinds of birds during the migratory season.

Canoes were not used much in the Loucheux country as the Loucheux generally travelled by dog sleigh. There was very little birch in the region and for their craft the natives used spruce. A good straight tree was selected and the bark notched at the top and bottom. First a narrow strip was removed, then wide strips were carefully lifted off with a stick pointed at one end like a chisel. The bark was then folded in two. The ends, bow and stern, were sewn on the inside with *watap* (roots of spruce trees). Knot holes, where branches occurred, were patched and covered with spruce gum mixed with oil and pitch. A wood frame (gunwale) was placed around this shaped bark, and two or three bars for lifting it placed horizontally across the top. Rough paddles or poles were made for steering. These canoes weren't much better than rafts. They were used chiefly for crossing streams, but were no good for travelling upstream.

CHAPTER 11

A Link with Franklin

During my years in charge of Fort Rae, I met many wonderful Indian hunters and noted guides including Old Chief Akaitcho, also called Chief Confidante, who had guided Franklin[8] to the polar sea. He was a wonderful old fellow.

Confidante was chief of a large band of Indians that came to my post to trade. The French named them *jeunes de large* (young men from out in the country). They were called Dogribs. It is said they got their name from a legend relating their descent from a dog and because they dried the ribs and sides of caribou for winter food. They were honest, hardworking men and an extremely important band of hunters whose hunting ground extended some three hundred miles out on the Barren Lands.

Confidante and his band seldom came to the fort more than once a year. The old chief was something of a fur trader himself. From the border of his territory, he used to send out runners to meet and trade with the Eskimo who were just beginning to venture south to trade with the Company. When business with the Eskimo was good, Confidante sent his runners to Fort Rae for extra supplies.

The Dogribs used every part of the caribou—hide, hair, meat, and bones. The horns they made into spears, handles for knives, and big spoons, like ladles. As an experiment, I sent a case of muskox horns to England, though the Company objected to the cost of transportation. Next year when the mail arrived from England, I was requested to send more. They were used in England for the manufacture of various utensils. These horns were difficult to transport—a pair weighed from fifteen to twenty pounds.

The Yellowknife Indians, a party of twenty able hunters, also came to my post to trade. They supplied all our muskoxen, otter skins, and other furs. They were good men but hard to deal with. Then we had a band called Jimmie's Brigade, who were good boatmen and fine fellows as well as excellent moose and deer hunters. They hunted within an area of 150 miles east and northeast of Fort Rae. This band visited my post twice a year, at Easter and Christmas. They were attached to the Roman Catholic mission and were more or less educated.

We had many sad accidents among the hunters and it was my business to attend to the injured. Everything that interrupted the work of the hunters interfered with our volume of trade. One fall I equipped Keskoray (Frozen Foot), who was a famous deer and moose hunter, with ammunition and provisions. He set off in his canoe with his wife and children, including his young son of fifteen, who was becoming a good hunter. At the hunting ground Keskoray made camp, then took the boy ten or twelve miles away to a channel connecting two lakes which was edged with grass. At dusk, the hunters crept through the grass to watch for moose or deer to come to drink. Hearing a beaver slapping his tail, plunging into the water and gnawing wood, they edged along. Keskoray thought the beaver was at the far end of the lake. He told the boy to remain where he was while he crept along to shoot the beaver.

Keskoray reached the lake end, but the beaver was gone. The boy, disregarding his father's orders, followed along on the opposite side of the water. Keskoray, hearing the noise, thought it was the beaver and when the boy lifted his head to peer through the grass, he fired. Keskoray went to pick up the dead animal and found his son with his head almost shot off. It was a terrible shock to the poor fellow. He picked up the dead boy and carried him on his back to camp, through the dark, cold night, singing the death song of his people.

Keskoray's wife, hearing the death chant, went out to meet her husband and her dead boy. Keskoray said, "I don't want to live! Here is my gun. Shoot me!" She succeeded in persuading him that the accident was not his fault. She was a strong woman. She carried the boy the rest of the way to camp.

The next day we were alarmed to hear Keskoray singing the death song as he came across the water. I took him and his wife out to my kitchen and did everything possible to console them both. My men made a coffin for the body and we buried the boy near the fort. The priest held burial service. I had to place a temporary guard of two men over Keskoray to keep him from killing himself. Keskoray was my chief hunter all the years I was at Fort Rae. I was very fond of him and his boy.

There were many other sad affairs at Fort Rae. We had a lame Indian who had got hurt in a hunting accident. One spring, just as the ice was breaking up, I sent a hunting party after the great flocks of geese and ducks that had arrived to breed on the islands. The lame chap was a good canoe man and he went with them. When the hunters separated, he wandered off to another island to collect eggs. He wasn't missed by the party until evening. In the morning the party found his canoe drifting and his body in the water. He had apparently slipped on the slimy rocks and hit his head. It was too far to bring his body to the fort so the hunters buried it temporarily on the mainland in the sand, covering it well with driftwood and stones.

When the accident was reported to me, I sent men to bury the body properly. They found the logs which they had laid over the grave burned and the body charred. The hunters had not put their campfire out properly and it had set fire to the driftwood. They put the charred body into a grave on the mainland and reported back to me. A week later the priest at the post sent boatmen to bring the body back for burial. It had been dug up and eaten. In spite of the priest, the Indians believed the evil Manitou had eaten the body.

I often went hunting with my men. Once on a trip after deer with Capot, I wounded one, and I had to follow it for an hour before I succeeded in killing it. By this time I was far from camp and Capot. It was almost dark so I decided to make a little fire and spend the night where I was. As my blanket and grub were with Capot, I decided to skin my deer and use the hide for a robe.

Wrapped in the skin, fur side next me, I went comfortably to sleep. I awoke in the morning imprisoned in a cocoon. I had to work and thresh about for some time before I finally got the frozen skin soft enough to release me. I had a breakfast of deer meat, took the deer tongue, and went back to the fort.

The wife of my interpreter, William Hoole, was a great hunter. She had her own gun. This meant that she was pretty highly regarded as a hunter. When the deer began arriving at Fort Rae, I always sent her on a little hunting expedition of her own to a deer pass in a valley at the other end of the mountain. I gave her some ammunition, for which I made no charge, and what meat she needed from the deer she shot; the rest came to the fort.

I was out with the fort hunters once when Mrs. Hoole, who was by herself in the same pass, killed nine deer, more than we did. As she killed a deer, she pulled it away out of sight and waited for another to come. I did not lose anything by giving her ammunition.

It was June 1868. Fort Rae was quiet. There was little business at the inland posts of the Company during the summer, for the Indians would not be back from their outer hunting grounds until the middle or last of August. A clerk could handle the trade and usually did. This year I was not required to accompany the summer brigades. Time lay heavy on my hands—but not for long. The fort hunters brought word that the caribou would be returning from the seacoast, and Chief Confidante (Akaitcho) of the Yellowknives and his band were moving into the Barren Lands. It would soon be time for the great annual caribou hunt, they said, and they ought to be off.

I was in a quandary. Wise and capable officers had preceded me at Fort Rae. As first officer of a great hunting region I should know at first-hand the territory tributary to my post and the hunting methods of the Indians. Both the post and Indian hunters were shrewd and experienced, yet it was my duty to encourage them to bring in more and more game. Here, deep in the interior of the country, I *was* the Company.

"Pack an outfit," I told the men. "I will go with you to join Akaitcho and his party. Set out two canoes, men's size; I will go as passenger in one with two Indians; two Indians will man the other."

The men soon had the outfit ready. In each canoe we packed one hundred pounds of trading goods: powder, shot, tobacco, cotton, and flannel. My own outfit consisted of a double-barrel gun, a revolver (five shot), ammunition (two pounds), five bags fine steel flint and punk, wax matches in a bottle, compass and burning glass (small), medicine box, Bible, pencil, paper, a six-ounce canvas sheet (to cover my bedding, act as tent, sail, or awning, even as mosquito net), a medium-size axe, knife, small copper kettle, small fry pan, two tin cups, two tin plates, fork, spoon, some pieces of birch bark for repairing canoes, a lot of gum, one dozen fishhooks, a short net (8 fths), blanket and raincoats, mitts, moccasins, cap and mosquito veil, hunting bag, tracking line, and portaging strap. Each man had his own personal baggage—about ten pounds.

We set out the middle of June. Encouraged by a nice leading wind, we strapped our canoes together and sailed (using our six-ounce duck sheets for sails) the twenty miles from Fort Rae to the main body of Great Slave Lake, camping that night at Big Point, the entrance to the lake. On the second day, the wind was stronger, so each canoe travelled singly. On all sides were rocky islands alive with nesting birds: ducks, gulls, loons—a great variety. We visited some of these islands long enough to collect a supply of eggs, some fresh, others not. I ate the fresh eggs; the stale ones were greatly enjoyed by my Indians. For fresh meat, we picked off a fine moose that crossed our path swimming between two islands. When we camped that night on a well-wooded island, the men prepared and packed enough moose meat for our immediate needs.

On the third day the wind was rough, but by keeping close to the mainland, we were able to make good time. That night we made camp at the headwaters of the Yellowknife River, approximately northeast of Fort Rae. On all sides of us were rocks. All day we had to fight a swift current and in many places, rather than risk taking our canoes over the rocks and rapids, we had made short portages. In high water the Yellowknife is a fair-sized river with many rapids and cascades and a strong current. The country it crosses is rocky with little or no timber. It was an excellent mixed-fur country and the only real muskox country in the Mackenzie River area.

For two more days we fought rapids, strained over portages, endured cascades. We had sufficient provisions—game, eggs, and fish—so we paid no attention to hunting. Poling, wading, tracking, stumbling—it was rough travelling. The portages were short, not more than five miles at the longest. The men carried their canoes and loads across on one trip; the weight for each man was two hundred pounds. A hunter tied his paddles lengthwise to the bars of his canoe, poked his rat spear and a nice pole—eight feet long and as thick as a man's wrist and smoothly knifed—in with them. He packed his dunnage on his back, his gun in his belt (the long guns were inconvenient to carry since they dragged), threw his canoe crosswise on his shoulders, and suspended it from his forehead by a carrying strap, keeping it steady with his hand.

A man can carry a canoe and make better time than a man walking without a load. He walks with a lambray step, half gliding. Not difficult at all, for once he gets started the weight of his load sends him gliding along. An able-bodied man can easily portage five miles without spelling. Generally, the men took a chew of tobacco and lambrayed along.

So, by a series of portages from land to rivers to lakes we advanced, always on the lookout for Chief Confidante's party. On the evening of the fifth day we came to a camp of Yellowknife: twelve able-bodied men, their wives, children, old people, and a pack of dogs. They received us warmly. We were the Company and had trading goods.

We spent two days with these people, who were striking northeastward to join Chief Confidante. We joined the party. The able hunters and the responsible young men formed into scouting parties and went out in a different direction in search of their chief and his principal hunting party. Now we were right in the so-called Barrens. Here, at this season, were flowers and mosses of many varieties, wild fruit, and birds of many kinds. I saw ducks, cranes, migratory geese—half a dozen kinds—chicken, ptarmigan, owls, and pelicans. We found here a peculiar little animal, native to the region, called a whistler or coney. The hills were riddled with them and they were easily caught. They would save a man from starvation, but I didn't care for the flavour, which was not as palatable as muskrat. The flies were fearful, but mosquitoes took the prize. For several days we followed the tracks of muskoxen.

I saw living muskoxen for the first time on this trip. It was at the headwaters of the Yellowknife. We had come upon a dozen females with their calves (born in May) and two bulls, a bull in charge of each six cows. Always when the calves are small, the females graze about amongst the rocks, keeping close to the valleys and avoiding open ground. The bulls stay on the high ground and maintain a sharp lookout for danger. I learned from my guides that muskoxen paw round holes in the ground, through the snow, and deposit their young in them. Snow and ice form a crust or shell over the calf. This protects it until it becomes strong enough to walk. To feed her calf, the mother stands over this shell, and the baby pokes its head to nurse through the hole or funnel formed by its warm breath.

The shooting of muskoxen when the female had young was a cruel practice to be discouraged. A mother will never leave her calf, and bulls will defend their families to the finish. These animals are handicapped by having short legs which prevent them from being able to run fast. On this trip, my hunters took only twenty muskoxen. Good Indian hunters never killed a whole herd, but left enough for breeding purposes. They showed excellent judgment in this respect, better than white men. They felt proud that the country and the animals in it belonged to them. Also, they knew that to clear the country of animals was to face hunger.

After several days' scouting, one of the Yellowknives found the track of the old Chief's band. He returned speedily with the news. I sent a runner forward to tell Confidante of our approach. The rest of our party followed. Timber wolves were bad. In the Barren Lands they travelled in bands; in the timber country, singly. Here on the border of the Arctic Circle, there were three varieties: white on the edge of the ice; on the Barren Lands proper they were a smaller animal; in the Strong Woods country they were called Strong Wood wolves and they were darker in colour.

These bands of wolves made no attempt to attack us. One big fellow, however, came within our range and one of our guides shot him. The skin of this wolf was different from any other wolf skin that I had taken in trade. It was lighter in colour than ordinary wolf—a dirty grey colour—and in the middle of the shoulders there were beautiful streaks of dark hair. These were the first coast wolves I had seen.

Always in the North, the guides carried their provision bags on their backs. They never thought of throwing them on the dogsleds. The reason was that a guide or hunter might leave the party in pursuit of game and lose his way. In their bags, besides a little food, they carried a pair of spare moccasins and some ammunition. It was a tradition amongst the Barren Lands tribes to carry a little food against starvation. Even the children were taught to carry a bit of food in bags.

After some days, we met my runner returning with a message from the chief, who had received him with dignity. He had been commanded to say that an officer of the Company would be well received.

At this time we fell in with a party of Dogribs, subject to Confidante. They were on their way to join the chief on his caribou hunt. Our average speed, travelling as we were, was twenty miles a day. Our general direction was east, but we were going from Fort Rae and the Coppermine River almost due east. By the time we reached the hunting ground of the Yellowknives, fifteen days later, we had come 250 miles from Fort Rae.

Confidante greeted me with respect and the right amount of cordiality. He had a tent pitched for my comfort and he commanded his people to attend me. We met as equals. It was seldom that Chief Akaitcho was called anything but Chief Confidante. This was the name given him by Franklin, whom he had accompanied in search of the Arctic Sea, as guide. Confidante was so named because Franklin had had confidence in the chief's ability and integrity.

The old chief was now nearing ninety. He had with him five of his thirty wives; the oldest was eighty years, the youngest was thirty. Both he and his old wife were travelling in state, as passengers. No English king ever received greater homage from his people. Special carriers attended him and his old wife and their baggage. Haste must be made to That-Mar, the crossing place of the caribou, he said, as it was close to the date of their arrival.

Our dogs hauled our goods—we had packs of furs and meat now—over the dry portages. Sometimes on the trail these huskies fought. These fights, though often serious, were comical too—the dogs with packs strapped to their backs dashing back and forth and getting tangled. We had hardships on that trip, but these were outweighed by the thrill of adventure. I was young and strong, and I was seeing a wild new country.

That-Mar (the crossing place) at last! Here the old chief chose a suitable spot for himself and his family and their attendants. Then he divided the party, partnering the young hunters with the able-bodied, and sending them to key points of observation to watch for the arrival of the herds.

From the old chief I learned the habits of caribou. At the end of August the males had gone to the edge of the timber to meet the females who were returning from the seacoast to winter in the Horn Mountains—about eighty miles across Great Slave Lake from That-Mar. After forming into one big herd, they travelled together for about a month. This was the breeding season. The males had full horns. Never were they later at That-Mar, the narrows at Great Slave Lake, than the first of November. It was as if they had a calendar, they were so regular. The males had stayed in the Strong Woods while the females had gone to the seacoast to have their young—away from flies and wolves. Nature protected the females. In summer the scent of their hooves disappeared, while that of the males remained to draw the attention of wolves.

At last the leader of the herd was sighted. He approached the edge of the water cautiously, then plunged swiftly in. As if this was a signal, the great plunging herd came like an avalanche after him. When they were well in the lake, the hunters divided. One half of the party shot their canoes out and alongside the animals and attacked; the others followed close to cut the caribou off from land. Caught between two attacking groups, the animals became confused and milled round and round. Right into them the hunters drove their canoes—even right up on the backs of the terrified animals. It was an astonishing spectacle. Canoes balanced on the backs of caribou, and in them hunters on their knees spearing right and left. And what spears! They were from six to nine feet long, with barbed heads. It required great skill to drive a spear directly into the kidney of an animal and withdraw it before it flinched and upset the canoe. An animal stabbed in the kidney gave a few kicks and died at once.

It was a terrible slaughter. The hunters killed thousands of caribou. Each year it had been the same. Skeletons of caribou lined the shores of That-Mar Crossing like driftwood fences. Not all the meat killed this day was saved; from some of the animals, only the tongues were taken. Following the hunt, there was a great dressing of skins. Skins of the female animals were used for making clothes. Leather and babiche was made from the male skins. The fawn skins were reserved for making children's clothing and underclothing. These people wore underclothing with the fur side next the skin.

I could not help advising the Yellowknives to preserve as much meat as possible from the hunt by drying it, putting the bones aside for soup, and preserving every bit of fat. Hearing this, Chief Confidante said, "For long I have been telling my people that white men, and Franklin, told me that all the meat should be saved."

The Company hunters alone killed about four hundred caribou. We preserved all the meat. Another hunting party sent out from the post killed more animals than we did, but they did not preserve as much meat.

Before leaving That-Mar, I traded the remaining stock of goods with Chief Confidante's eldest son. In return, he agreed to bring furs to the fort when convenient. And so I bade goodbye to the old chief. He was sere as a yellow leaf. I left him to the warmth of his blankets.

CHAPTER 12

With the Sir Sanford Fleming Expedition

In 1871 Mr. William Lucas Hardisty granted me leave of absence for the one season—one outfit—with full pay on account of the illness of my father. He gave me a letter to Mr. Donald Smith, his brother-in-law, which he let me read. He said, "These two young Englishmen, Julian Stewart Onion (Camsell) and W. C. King, officers serving under me, are men who will maintain the prestige of the Hudson's Bay Company." Onion later changed his name in the Company's books to Camsell, his family name.

When I was in Montreal on my way back from England—after my leave from Fort Rae—I met Governor James Grahame. He said, "See here, King, your aunt in British Columbia, Mrs. Bishop Hill, is a friend of my wife's. She wants you to be transferred to Victoria, B.C. When you reach Fort Garry, pick up Sanford Fleming's party, and take them on across Canada. See that they have provisions and travelling accommodation."

When I reached Fort Garry, Donald A. Smith ordered me to the Victoria post via Edmonton. I picked up the Sanford Fleming expedition at Fort Garry and travelled with them across the plains. The trip was pleasant. On Sundays we stopped to let the men wash their clothes and mend their harnesses and carts.

My duty was to see that the party got every assistance from the Hudson's Bay posts en route, and to send the accounts back to Fort Garry.

Buffalo were scarce but we shot enough as we travelled to keep us supplied with fresh meat. I always took part with the men in their buffalo forages. One day, two or three of the men and some Cree Indians whom we met went after a small herd. I got separated from the party and seeing a lone buffalo, went after him. To my amazement the beast stood stock still though I fired several shots into him. When I rode up, I discovered that the beast was dead.

Shot by the hunters and in pain, he had evidently braced his short legs outward like pegs and they had become rigid and supported him. He was braced very substantially and his heavy head hung between his forelegs. I poked him with my gun and he fell over.

The only thing for me to do was to stay where I was in the hope that Fleming would send a search party out to look for me. Night came. I was hungry, thirsty, and desperately cold. For warmth I pressed up against the thick, shaggy coat of my buffalo and listened to the coyotes howl. In the morning the searchers found me. My experience with the dead buffalo provided great jollity for the party.

Fleming's son, a college youth, was with the party officially as cook—he had a cook to do the actual cooking—but he was required to help his father run survey lines. The boy wasn't much good at this work so I took his place and enjoyed it.

When we parted, Fleming asked me to get in touch with him whenever I happened to be in Ottawa, saying that he would be glad to help me in any way he could in the Company. Naturally we had discussed the unjust methods of promotion in the service— mainly that those officers who had not married the daughters of factors had little chance of advancement in the service, as only the governor had the power to promote a man and his decision was governed by family votes. I saw Fleming sometime later in Ottawa—at his invitation—and he asked me to write a letter expressing my views, in an effort to right injustices to other men as well as myself, and he'd take the matter up with the Board[9] in England. This he did, but it only resulted in Canadian criticism of my act.

Fleming was a fine fellow. He did what he could for me. He knew that my people in England were trying to get me out of the service, offering to set money aside for me ... but, funny thing, when they came to die, they left me nothing.

At Edmonton, I left the Sanford Fleming party and joined Harrison Young and another clerk who were on their way to British Columbia by way of the Peace River, travelling with carts and pack horses. At Peace River, Dunvegan, we met the Chipewyan boat brigade, in charge of Ferdinand Mackenzie, on its way back to Chipewyan. It had come from exchanging cargoes with the Leather Party (Coast Indians), who had already left on their return trip. Now, we couldn't get to British Columbia. I joined the brigade to Fort Chipewyan.

On our way to the North, Chief Factor William McMurray, who was in charge of the Athabaska Post, asked Hardisty to take Nichol Sinclair, a clerk, off his hands. When Hardisty proposed that I take him to Mackenzie's river, I said I had only one dogsled. McMurray said, "Sinclair is a noted runner and will walk and run ahead of the dogs."

Sinclair was a harum-scarum sort of a fellow. He was in love with my wife's sister, Ellen Flett. I agreed to take him, and put his baggage on my sled. He started running smartly at the rate of around eight miles an hour. I went at my usual travelling gait, overtaking Sinclair halfway over the long portage, tired and perspiring. Better take it easy, I told him, as we had a trip of from five to eight hundred miles ahead of us, on foot, but he insisted on going six or seven miles further at the same fast rate. When I came up to him again, he was sitting on a lump of ice nursing a cramp in his leg. He wasn't dressed properly for running or travelling. His shoes were small and the strings tight. After another mile of running, he broke into a walk. My dogs passed him. Sinclair began to fall behind. Cameron, who was following me with his dogs, wouldn't give him a ride. When I looked back, Sinclair was limping. I checked my dogs, waited for him, and told him to jump on the sled and have a smoke. A little further on we stopped and made a cup of tea. Sinclair's leg grew worse. He had sprung it and couldn't walk a step. I had to haul him all the way to Fort Smith.

We stopped at Old Beaulieu's place. He treated us decently and gave us good meals. I got Nichol off in the morning. I left him at Fort Resolution and did not see him again for a year. He was later sent to Hay River to establish a little post, where he built a small store and some small houses for the Company. The Fort Providence Indians traded with him.

Time passed. One day at Fort Chipewyan, on the first ice, some Indians came to my post to report that the clerk at Hay River was starving. His hunters hadn't returned and he had lost all his nets in storms and high winds. Nichol Sinclair wasn't much good about managing. He was a fine fellow in some respects, but always in trouble. I set off with provisions for him, after notifying Hardisty of the situation, and got him fixed up temporarily. Eventually he landed at Ile-à-la-Crosse. The Company made it easy for him to retire from the service.

Then he astonished us all. He started a trading business at Green Lake in opposition to the Company, getting a good quantity of furs and causing us trouble.

My original orders from Hardisty, when I took my furlough, were to return to the Mackenzie River District. When I arrived at Fort Chipewyan, Chief Factor William Christie was surprised. MacFarlane had told him he had arranged with Richard Hardisty for me to go to Fort Rae. My explanation of the circumstances that had landed me at Fort Chipewyan wasn't enough. Christie required a written statement from MacFarlane to forward to headquarters at Fort Garry. I had too many people interested in my welfare. I was finally kept at Fort Chipewyan, second in command to MacFarlane. I remained there for two winters—1872–73.

While I was at Fort Chipewyan, Major William Butler, afterwards Sir William, came to the post. He had been wintering north of Prince Albert at Snake Plains.

MacFarlane had to be away on inspections a good deal, so during the week of Butler's stay, I was official host. Butler spent most of his time with the Catholic priest, the Indians, and John MacRae and Jimmie Spencer of our staff, who could inform him about the country. Moberly, of Fort McMurray, visited the post that week, so altogether Butler got considerable information. MacFarlane was of course his most important and authoritative source of information.

One day an Indian hunter reported to me that his party had killed some buffalo thirty-five miles across the Peace River. I was short of men, so I sent John MacRae, the young clerk, with

Harper, a Red River Métis—Butler called him "Harper of the villainous countenance"—to get the meat.

The men took two sleds. MacRae was a greenhorn and it was his first trip with dogs. The Indian runners took the men safely to the meat, but on their return across Lake Claire, some fifteen miles from the fort, MacRae fell behind, driving the sled. Harper was on ahead of the dogs. A snowstorm came and it began to drift. Harper hurried on and soon outdistanced the dogsled. The drift grew so thick that MacRae lost sight of Harper and in the storm the dogs lost Harper's scent. After a time Harper missed the sled, but he carried on till he struck land, where he made a fire and spent the night. In the morning he hurried on to the fort. My men ran to tell me that Harper had come without MacRae. I sent for him, and after he had explained the circumstances, I blamed him for leaving the green clerk behind. Harper said MacRae would have caught up if the storm hadn't separated them. Well, the law of the North was every man for himself. Experienced men were used to taking responsibility for themselves and made no allowances for greenhorns. I couldn't say much.

I immediately sent four men and two Indians after MacRae. A little later I sent out another search party. The men found MacRae's sled where he had placed his pushing stick in the ice for a marker. From the sled, they tracked MacRae nearly six miles before finding him in a dazed condition walking directly away from the fort. His hands and feet were badly frostbitten.

The men made camp, fed him, and let him sleep. Two of the runners returned to the fort to report to me, travelling all that day and night. I sent a cariole back for MacRae.

MacRae said that after losing sight of Harper he had struck a willow point and made a little fire of rushes. All the next day he had wandered. On the third day, he had unharnessed the dogs and they left him. If he had given the dogs the lead, they would have brought him to the fort. When the weather cleared, he saw some hills and thought them close. He was making for them when the men found him. The hills were thirty miles away.

A few days after MacRae's rescue, MacFarlane returned. Between us, we made Harper realize the importance of guides taking the responsibility for green men not used to the dangers and hardships of northern travel. MacRae recovered, but after a time his mind became unbalanced. I had great trouble preventing him from injuring himself. We sent him back to Scotland. His father was a Scottish minister.

Butler was a very agreeable companion. His plan was to go up the Peace River and across the mountains. MacFarlane accompanied him for some distance north.

There was a shortage of furs this year, but luckily prices on the London market were high. Suddenly, we discovered that we were threatened with sharp opposition. Into our territory came the trading partners Colin Fraser, Henry Fraser, McGillis, and McQuestion. They were important free traders at Battleford and Prince Albert, and were giving us a lot of bother. McGillis's right-hand man was La Ronde. We couldn't break McGillis, but we eventually bought him partly out.

I spent most of that winter travelling through the district, getting to Indian camps ahead of these free traders and buying up the furs. I used to say to MacFarlane, "Give me the money and the prestige of the Company and I'll oppose these free traders successfully every time!"

As for the free traders, they said, "King is the darndest fellow the Company has ever sent against us! He doesn't care for anything so long as he gets the furs!" My secret was to buy every fur and never mind the expense.

According to the Company system, a skin was a certain price, whether prime or not. After they had been assorted, however, they had a vastly different value. In the civilized (London) market, a dark, extra large, well-preserved skin had a special value. In the fur market beaver skins were not sold by weight but separately. A dark beaver pelt was worth four or five times more than a pale beaver. This was my system of valuation in trading. Now this system is altered.

In the summer of 1873 I made a trip with the brigade from Fort Chipewyan to Fort McMurray. Mr. Hardisty was in charge of the boats with their cargoes of furs to P.L.L., as we called Portage La Loche. Friction arose between the boatmen and the steersman and the Indian crew rebelled.

Mr. Hardisty noticed by his almanac that an eclipse of the sun was due. The day before the predicted eclipse, Hardisty warned the Indians that unless they obeyed orders the sun would darken and the world go black. He said, "If you refuse to get into the boats and continue on this trip, I will end the world tomorrow."

The rebellion continued. Next day, when we put ashore for lunch, on came the eclipse. The terrified Indians rushed to the boats. In their panic, they wanted to go back instead of forward, but Hardisty gave them tobacco and persuaded them to have a smoke and keep quiet. He said he would arrange with the Big Manitou to postpone the ending of the world. As they sat smoking, the eclipse ended. "*Ta-pwa-a-chee!*" cried the Indians. "It is true that the master has influence with the Manitou!" We continued on our trip without further trouble.

In the year 1874, I was married to Charlotte Flett. Alex La Ronde fiddled at my wedding.

As the records attest, I married myself, at Fort Chipewyan, to Charlotte Flett, on August 4, 1874. And no marriage was more truly performed in the sight of God. I was remarried to Charlotte Flett by Civil Contract, with witnesses, by Mr. R. MacFarlane, J.P., in August 1874, on his first visit to the post after my marriage. Our child, my son W. H. King, was born on July 3, 1875. Rev. Mr. Shaw remarried us in 1875, at the time he christened my son, in September 1875. The church ceremony was to please my wife. So I have married three times.

My wife's father, George Flett, was a boat builder for the Company. He had built the boats, at Fort Vermilion, for Lieutenant Lefroy of the British navy, who had spent the winter there preparing an expedition to go in search of Franklin. This was about 1850. George Flett got one of the medals issued by the British government to all those who took part in or helped prepare for the relief expedition.

After my marriage in 1874, I was sent immediately to take charge of Fort St. John. Accompanying my wife and me to Fort St. John—in another boat—were Donald Ross, Alexander (Black) Mackenzie, and two young clerks: Webster, an Englishman, and Count Alstoff Beneke, a Belgian. They were on their way to the British Columbia post. Beneke was related to the King of Belgium. He was an agreeable young fellow. He had spent the winter at Fort Qu'Appelle under Archibald Macdonald. The only thing celebrated about him, however, was his big nose. He had acted as groomsman at my wedding. My wife had made a pair of beautifully embroidered mitts. These I gave to Beneke for a gift. My new wife felt a little hurt about it.

Near St. John, we put ashore for breakfast. Here the banks of the Peace are five or six hundred feet high. My steersman, John Courte Oreilles (French for cut or short ears) noticed some bears on the top of the hill. Through the glasses we made out five. Two were sitting on their haunches, peering through the bushes.

Beneke always carried a fancy revolver. He wanted to get a shot at the grizzlies. Courte Oreilles said to me, "I am going to send some of the boatmen ashore to shoot the bears." I agreed, warning him not to let his men stay too long. I called to Beneke to go with the men if he wanted to. He was delighted. Through my glasses, I watched the men land across the river. Two of them ran along the beach upstream, two downstream. Beneke went crawling up the steep hill to get a shot at the bears. He got slowly upward. One of the bears strolled away; the other sat watching Beneke creep up. When he was within twenty yards of the bear, Beneke fired. There was a little puff of smoke. The bear scratched himself. Beneke kept on firing, the bear scratching. Beneke's little shots only stung the bear. Soon his cartridges gave out. The bear made a leap downhill. Beneke took to his heels. The bear missed Beneke, turned the wrong way, and was shot by two boatmen who were on the watch. The other men got two of the bears. I had to admire Beneke for facing uphill to a bear with only a revolver. I left Beneke and Webster at Hudson's Hope. After a few years in the country visiting about at posts, Beneke left the country. Webster could carve anything with a pocket knife. He spent several years in the country, then went to Australia.

I had to stop at Hudson's Hope,[10] where I met two old Cornish miners who had arrived from Finlay River. They carried packs and rifles and they had a little gold. One of them, an extraordinary looking character, wore a fur cap. He said that as they were coming along the trail, single file, he heard a huff-huff in front of him and when he looked up there was a bear sitting on his haunches. He had poked his gun into the bear's mouth and shot him. He said I could have the carcass. I sent two men with pack horses after it. I was surprised when they returned with a grizzly. I gave the miners five dollars in cash and six dollars worth of grub for it, then completed my work at Hudson's Hope and continued on my journey.

At Fort St. John, miners were constantly passing to and fro. I often watched these fellows washing gold along the riverbank. They would walk along the beach, observing the sandbars, and when a bar looked good they would throw a stick into the river. If it drifted to the sandbar gold was indicated. A favourite place for washing gold was two or three miles above St. John. A miner could wash from four dollars to five dollars worth of gold a day, but this he did not consider profitable as his daily provisions at my post cost him about the same amount. These gamblers would keep moving from bar to bar until they washed up to ten dollars a day. When their returns were less than three dollars they moved on to Dunvegan.

One of these fellows left his gold washing outfit, rocker, and quicksilver at my post, so I decided to try my hand at gold washing. In three hours, I secured enough gold lumps to fill a tobacco jar. I crushed these lumps, miner fashion, to the size of a pipe bowl and put them away. One day, sometime later, when I was travelling with Professor Macoun, I told him about my gold washing and showed him my gold lump. He said it had some value and offered to have it fixed up for me when he should return to Ottawa. I gave him the gold and forgot about it. I was greatly surprised when he sent me a pair of spectacle frames and a ring made out of it.

George Kennedy had preceded me in charge of the St. John post, though I had had charge of it for a short time the previous year. Then, when the outlaw "Nigger" Dan came into the district from the United States and began setting fires, stealing cordwood, getting furs illegally from the Indians, and causing the Company to lose business, MacFarlane said, "I'll send King up there!"

"Nigger" Dan tried to terrorize me, too. When I found out that he was stealing my cordwood, I took the tops off bullets, filled them with gunpowder, and inserted them into the wood. Then, unobserved, I watched "Nigger" Dan in his little shack put this wood in his fire. The explosion blew his chimney to pieces. It's a wonder he wasn't killed. He left his shack and made camp outside, but he continued stealing my cordwood. Again his fire exploded and the shock knocked him over.

Presently I learned that he was spreading poison for my dogs. I discovered too that he was picking the mud from between the logs of my store and taking the pemmican strips that were stacked against the wall. I put some strychnine and croton oil into the meat.

A week later, I heard terrible groaning in Dan's shack. An old fellow, La Flume, came running to tell me that "Nigger" Dan was rolling in agony and wanted me. I didn't go as I thought he intended to shoot me, but I gave La Flume some epsom salts, a vomit, and a purgative powder for the sufferer.

"Nigger" Dan got better and stopped stealing my meat, but one day, sometime later, I was standing at the door of my house having a smoke when a bullet whizzed past my head, just missing me. I went up to my little garret window and banged back at "Nigger" Dan. This scared him a bit.

Soon after this little exchange of shots, I returned to my house one day to find "Nigger" Dan telling my wife how cruel I was. She told him that he had deserved punishment. Well, he agreed to a truce of friendship with me and we had no further trouble. After I left Fort St. John, he was arrested for another offence.

I Entertain the Geological Survey Party

In the spring of 1875, I was on my way to Hudson's Hope with a load of moose skins and to get supplies when I met a geological survey party coming down the Finlay River to Fort St. John. The party, in charge of Professor A. R. C. Selwyn, included Arthur Webster, Professor Selwyn's assistant, Professor Macoun, a botanist, a cook, and a campman. Their outfit consisted of a big canoe, a canvas boat on a frame, and a birch bark canoe.

I met the party at Hell's Gate, at the rapid the Indians called Kinepalpas (the rapid that doesn't speak). It was Selwyn's camp smoke near the rapid that attracted me and I crossed the river to greet the travellers. My men had that morning killed a moose and a beaver, so I exchanged some meat with Selwyn for oatmeal, molasses, and a few other luxuries. I advised the party to go on to my post, saying that I would be back in ten days.

In going up the rapid to Hell's Gate that morning Michael, my steersman, had almost drowned. The Hell's Gate is a very dangerous rapid. On each side of the canyon the river cuts under the mountains and the current would ordinarily carry the canoe far under these banks. The canyon, or rapid, varies in width from 150 to 190 yards and is underlaid by rocks. To run this rapid, once with an important passenger, nine men were placed on each bank of the river—four men pulling on the lines attached to the canoe and one man to keep each line clear. The passenger sat in the middle of the canoe. The steersman had a man ready to clear the lines and fend the canoe off rocks. The bowman had a man to help him. When the trackers came to a particularly dangerous place, they pulled the lines so taut that the body of the canoe was almost lifted from the water. Michael was in the canoe, with two men on the tracking lines and, in going around the point, the current had caught the canoe. When this happens the lines must be loosened immediately or the canoe will upset. The men threw off the straps quickly enough, but the canoe swung over the rapid and upset. Michael was a powerful swimmer and was able to fight the rapid and get to shore. The canoe wasn't damaged much, but the furs were soaking. We had to spread our cargo out on the rocks to dry. I warned Selwyn about this rapid and we went on.

On the portage from Parsnip River to the Company's post at McLeod Lake, where Ferdinand Mackenzie was the clerk in charge, we met a woman dressed in man's clothing. She looked a regular huntress. She carried a fishing rod and basket, a rifle, and in her belt a pair of silver-mounted revolvers. She wore a black felt hat. It was unusual to see women dressed like this in the North (men wore toques, women wore head shawls). We spoke to her and learned that she was Mackenzie's wife, a Métis woman. We went on to the fort. In the evening Mrs. Mackenzie turned up. She was very entertaining. She played the fiddle and concertina. Before I left in the morning, she gave me a present of a four-barreled silver-mounted revolver. I went back to Fort St. John on horseback—about sixty miles.

When I arrived back at Fort St. John, I found Macoun busy collecting specimens of plants and Webster taking bearings of the river. Selwyn wanted to examine the canyon (cannel coal occurred here), but I said, "If you go monkeying around that canyon, you'll get drowned."

He laughed. "I'll risk it," he said.

"Well," I said, "if anything happens to your party I'll be blamed. In a way, you are under my protection. For one thing, your boats are unsuitable and your men untrained."

"If you have been there, I can go," he said.

There was no use pointing out that I was a seasoned and experienced boatman and he was a greenhorn. He was determined to go. "Then you must take one of my best boatmen," I said.

Next morning he started off, without the Indian guide I had assigned him. He didn't want the extra expense of a guide. An hour or two passed. I was busy in the store when a woman came running to tell me that Selwyn was drowning. I hurried out. The guide I had picked for Selwyn was a sensible fellow and, anticipating an accident, he had followed.

Selwyn's boatmen had got over the first cascade, but in attempting the second, the current gained on him and the canoe broadsided and upset. At this point the river is about two hundred yards wide and in the middle of it huge boulders divide the canyon, forming a boiling rapid.

I watched the struggle in the water. My man, who was a noted and expert canoe man, stood ready on the beach. When Selwyn came tumbling down the foaming rapid, my man shot out to the rock upon which Selwyn had been washed, snatched him just as another torrent swept him off again, and got him to shore. Selwyn's man managed to hang on to the overturned canoe. My man got both canoes and man ashore.

Selwyn was in pretty bad shape. We got him to bed and by the next morning he was able to show up for breakfast. He asked me as a special favour not to report the accident, but I explained that other than reporting the affair to the district officer, little need be said. We were quite a distance from the press in those days and our doings in the North did not receive much publicity. Selwyn paid the guide generously for saving his life.

It took the canoe men and trackers two days to run that thirty-six miles, although it was downstream. This was the canyon that Selwyn attempted. I sent samples of cannel coal from this canyon to the Smithsonian Institute.

From the hills, I often looked down at this raging roaring rapid. Animals going near it to drink were often caught in it and washed away. It was nothing to find deer, bear, wolves, and moose washed down the rapids.

After his mortifying experience, Selwyn decided to go up West Pine River to examine the pass through the mountains. His canoe was unfit to make the trip and carry three men, as he wished. I insisted on providing him with a good, safe canoe. I said: "You and two men will go in one canoe and Webster, the cook, and another man, in the other. I'll let you have old Coutereau (an old man almost eighty). He is an experienced guide and a perfect canoe man."

I got them off, Coutereau steering Selwyn's canoe aided by a Métis boatman. Webster followed more slowly with another steersman that I provided. Old Coutereau took Selwyn safely to where they had to leave the river and branch off to Summit Lake. He returned in about ten days.

During the absence of his chief, Macoun was busy collecting specimens. When Selwyn returned, he produced a peculiar plant and said to Macoun, "Professor, what's the name of this plant?"

I saw from the expression on Macoun's face that he was displeased. He asked Selwyn where he had found the plant. Selwyn replied that he had picked it up in his recent rambles.

The professor flew off the handle. "You never found this plant in this region. It does not grow on this side of the Rockies. You picked it up on the Pacific Coast and are testing me to see if I know my job. Your action is contemptible," he said.

Well, Selwyn and Macoun were pretty cool to each other after this. Later, when Selwyn said that he was going to return the way he had come, Macoun said, "I shall not go back with you. I'll go to Ottawa alone!"

Next day Selwyn and his party got off. Macoun remained at the post, collecting and preserving more plant specimens.

CHAPTER 14

Macoun and His Plants

Macoun dried and pressed his numerous specimens and mounted them in books. Sometime after Selwyn's departure, when I was going to Fort Chipewyan to meet the brigade, Macoun asked if he could accompany me. All my men were out hunting and they had the good canoes. The only thing I had at the post was a wretched dugout canoe. "I couldn't take you in this makeshift craft," I said. He insisted on making the trip, and I being a good-natured fellow, gave in. I made him write a testament for my files saying that he had insisted on coming with me and at his own risk.

I did not know how far we would have to travel before meeting the boat, so I took a little grub, some ammunition, and my flintlock gun. Macoun sat in the bow with a pole, trying to help with the steering. Our first 150 miles downstream brought us almost to Battle River. We shot a few beaver, ducks, and some other game as we went along.

One foggy morning as we drifted along, Macoun in the bow, I steering, we saw through the fog a bear on the shore drinking. The bear was only six or eight yards away and he was as surprised as we were. I grabbed my gun, dropped a ball into it, fired, and missed. The bear made a grab at me as the canoe swung past.

He missed me and ran along the beach. I loaded and started after him, but he got away.

The next day, we got to the Battle River trading post (an outpost of Fort Vermilion), which was a small place kept up by the Company. It was in charge of a clerk named John McCaulay. When I got opposite the mouth of the Battle River, I decided to run across and visit him. Thank heaven that I did. He and his family were starving. His men had gone with the boats, and the Indians tributary to his post hadn't come from their hunt. He himself was no hunter. For a month he and his family had been living on sap and pith from poplar trees and a few berries. They had eaten their parchment (rawhide) windows. The fellow was no good for the Peace River or Athabaska District. He was a Southern District man. He had no business in the North.

I fixed them up with all the game I had—beaver, ducks, geese, and some provisions—promising to send supplies from Vermilion. I learned afterwards that his hunters did not return until a week after my visit. I advised MacFarlane that McCaulay was no man for this isolated post. He was removed presently and the post abandoned.

Between the Battle River trading post and Vermilion I killed a moose and had most of the carcass in the canoe when I reached the Vermilion post. Macoun and I certainly had plenty of food. I found Mackenzie, the manager there, away in the boats to Chipewyan. He had left Mr. William Shaw, who was between eighty and ninety years of age, in charge of the post. Shaw lived to be a hundred. The Rev. A. C. Garrioch was the minister at Vermilion in Shaw's time, and probably the only man who knew what Shaw did with his diary. Shaw was a freeman, who married a Beaver Indian woman. He was a great old man. In his young days, before joining the Company, he had taught school at Fort Garry. Though a sort of pensioner, he was still capable and active, and a great writer. He had written an account of his experiences in the Peace River country, but at his death these records could not be found, nor have they turned up to this day. This regular and accurate account of the early happenings in the country would be of great value today. These old fellows all had a habit of hiding their records. Many of them have never been found.

It was at Vermilion that I learned from Mr. Shaw about the birth at Chipewyan of my little boy. I was greatly excited and naturally in a hurry to see him. I waited for nothing, but took some bannock, chopped meat, and potato (this was like dumpling) and got off.

We travelled on, expecting to meet the boat from Fort Chipewyan. Just before we reached the Boiling Rapid, Macoun said, "Look at that plant on the shore!" I couldn't see a sign of a plant. My eyesight was good. Few could fool me on quickness of observation. I didn't want to stop, but Macoun looked so disappointed that I ran the canoe ashore for a minute. By Jove! He found his plant. I still don't think he saw that plant, as he knew that it was native to the region, but used this ruse to get me ashore. Well, we both rejoiced over the plant. A fine fellow, Macoun.

This was about the middle of the day. Macoun said, "Can't we boil the kettle? I'll look for plants," and he was off. I put the kettle on the fire, picked up my gun, and went off to shoot a chicken for dinner and to eat some berries. In my absence Macoun returned to get something and, finding the fire low, piled some dry hay on to it. Off he went again after his plants. I looked back and saw a great smoke. The camp was on fire. All we saved was Macoun's box of specimens and my blanket. His blankets, which we had spread out on willows, and our other clothes were burned. Now we had to hurry away.

At tea time we went ashore. I shot three or four wood fowl. I was complaining because we had no tea. Macoun said, "China and Japan are pretty far away, but I'll give you some tea, some swamp muskeg tea." The natives used this. Off he went to a muskeg and got some. We boiled the flowers. It wasn't too bad at all, just slightly acrid in flavour. We made a very good meal on wood fowl and muskeg tea and got off again.

About fifteen miles below Vermilion, we came to the cascade across the river—a deadfall of eighteen to twenty feet—which was a miniature Niagara. Now I would have to shoot this cascade in my infernal canoe and with Macoun. He was a greenhorn, but I liked him. At the cascade navigation stops. There was a twenty-foot drop at ordinary water. About two miles before we reached this cascade, the current was so strong that it was almost impossible to make headway against it.

Anxious to see my wife and my new son, I decided not to waste time portaging the necessary two miles but to run to the very head of the cascade and so reduce the portage to two hundred yards. Before I reached the cascade, I decided to haul the canoe along the edge of the water over the rocks. I got Macoun out of the canoe, gave him a tracking line carefully rolled into a ball and directions to follow the shore, holding the line firmly and slackening or tightening it as I instructed. I warned him at the peril of his life not to drop the line lest I be washed over the rapid. I emphasized every possible danger. He promised to obey my instructions: not to drop the line, to keep the canoe hauled close to the beach.

In spite of my clear directions, I noticed that Macoun was holding the drop line carelessly. I stopped, tore a towel in two, wrapped it around the tracking strap, which wasn't any too strong, and tied it around his waist. All went well for one hundred yards. Then, my greenhorn slipped on the rocks and let go of the ball. I was washed out into the foaming current, heading for the cascade. Luckily I was able to cut the tracking line. Now I said a prayer and ran the canoe straight into the rapid, steering as best I could for some driftwood that had caught in the current. I leaped onto the driftwood. The canoe went over the fall. I managed to get ashore.

With my canoe went my blanket, gun, grub, and Macoun's dunnage, including his box of specimens. I had been carried far past Macoun in the current. On catching up to me, Macoun said, "My God, my specimens!" I felt pretty hot. "Damn your specimens!" I yelled. There is nothing more pitiful than a greenhorn.

Macoun had all the luck. When I finally got my canoe out of the swirling eddy, there was his specimen box wedged tight under the bow. All I possessed was gone. I was lucky indeed to get my canoe. We had nothing now to eat, and no gun or ammunition. All I had was my trousers and shirt.

From this point to the Company post at Little Red River— another outpost of Fort Vermilion—we made our way. Here we got a small outfit. This outpost was a little place provided for Baptiste Saint Crier, an old pensioner of the Company. It was under the direction of MacFarlane. McMurray was very fond of the old fellow and had provided this little trading station for him.

It took us three days to go from Little Red River to Quatre Fourches River (Four Forks River) a distance of twenty miles, which was ordinarily a day and a half's travel. It was a terrible job for one man in a dugout canoe and with a helpless passenger. We had little to eat. With a pole we killed game along the shore and speared jackfish. The unusual food made Macoun sick. Now I had to worry about him.

At Quatre Fourches River, we found all the men gone to meet the brigade at Chipewyan—eight miles distant. Two women were left in charge. They couldn't do much for us. The men had taken all the boats. At the end of that eight miles were my wife and child. I must get on! One of the old women let me take her daughter's birch bark canoe. It wasn't a canoe at all, but a thing that looked like a washing basket. It was used by the women for fishing along the shore. I decided to make the eight miles to Chipewyan in this craft. There was a strong wind off Lake Athabaska.

I arranged with the old women to put Macoun to bed. He was completely miserable. I started off about sunset. For three miles all went well, then the rising wind forced me to paddle along in the lee of shore—in the shelter of the islands. But in spite of this protection my almost-round canoe kept drifting and carrying me out of my course. About a mile and a half from the fort I struck great waves. It was pitch dark. I sang hymns. Gradually I mastered the waves and approached Fort Chipewyan. On the beach, fires flared brilliantly against the black. The Mackenzie's river brigade had arrived.

I saw lights in the clerk's window. My wife would be there. All at once I ran my washing basket right in amongst the lines of canoes. I jumped out and went to the house of my father-in-law to find out where my wife was. "She is here!" he said. My wife, carrying our baby, ran out. She had recognized my knock. In our excitement we let the baby fall, which greatly provoked my wife's mother.

"Why," I asked my father-in-law, "is my wife in your house and not where she belongs, in my room at the fort?" I went to find MacFarlane and inquire into the matter, after instructing my father-in-law to have my wife and boy and their belongings brought immediately to the fort.

Hardisty had to go to Mackenzie's river with the brigade. So MacFarlane asked me to stay at Chipewyan and go to Portage La Loche for supplies. The only boats available for the trip were two condemned transportation boats, and the only boatmen to man them were poor old men—just apologies for boatmen. All the good boatmen were elsewhere on trips. We could only carry a half-cargo—120 pieces in each boat.

I took Macoun. His plan was to get to Fort McMurray, proceed from there to Lac La Biche, then to Edmonton. Along the way, he collected samples of tar at the tar beds near Fort McMurray. At the fort, I put him off with his specimens. When I saw him at Fort Garry a year later, he was still talking about his plants.

At Portage La Loche I got my supplies and returned to Chipewyan. Those miserable boats! The seams were so dry that we had to keep caulking the holes continually with oakum and rags. They were certainly *not* Company style. MacFarlane welcomed us back with the cargo, which was badly needed. The men were amused when we appeared in our old craft with patched sails. MacFarlane said, "King, you always turn up when I am in a hole!"

No man in the service had better judgment and ability than Roderick Ross MacFarlane! He was a good post manager and trader. He collected valuable and rare specimens of plants and animals for the Smithsonian Institute in the United States, and gave the most competent and valuable assistance to professors of the institute who came into the country to conduct research.

He established a trading post (1860) in the Arctic which he named Fort Anderson, after Chief Factor James Lockhart Anderson, who discovered the Anderson and Lockhart rivers.

Chief Factor Anderson of Fort Simpson was in charge of the Mackenzie River District at the time of Sir John Franklin's expedition. He himself made overland trips in charge of rescue parties. He was a very able and distinguished Company officer. During his time he started all exploratory expeditions within the country, outfitting them and giving them reliable guides, provisions, and valuable geographical directions. His ideas, knowledge, and advice laid the foundation for the development of the Canadian North-West. Under him exploration was carried on by Camsell, Hardisty, and other officers. In addition to his great work in the development of the country, he laid the foundation for the successful carrying on of the business of the Company in Mackenzie's river.

After building Fort Anderson, MacFarlane received orders to abandon the post, as a plague had killed off practically all the Indians. He was collecting specimens for the Smithsonian Institute at the time. Some time later, in discussing the closing order with Hardisty and me, he said, "My collection wasn't complete and I had no intention of leaving the post before I got the specimens I wanted." Just when he had all the varieties he wanted and was preparing to close the post, he received instructions to continue the business. Pretending that he hadn't received them, he promptly closed the post. "Business just then did not warrant keeping the post open," he said.

About 1885, there was a great row between the wintering partners and the Board in England and, by agreement between the country officers, MacFarlane went to England to represent them. One of the partners' demands was for an increase in their salaries.

The Board asked MacFarlane to present written authority to speak for the other officers, but MacFarlane told them pretty forcefully that his word was sufficient authority. He made his demands in no uncertain terms. The arguments grew pretty hot. No man sitting in a London office, MacFarlane said, could tell him or the other partners how to run the fur business. He threatened to resign and work against the Company.

For this threat, the Board struck his name off the list. When he returned to the country and reported his dismissal, the other partners upheld his stand and demanded his reinstatement. The Board was forced to allow it, as they dared not oppose the power of the country managers of the Company.

He remained with the Company for eight years after this when, upon making further demands for the partners, he was retired on pension. MacFarlane was a power in the Company and influential enough to ruin it by starting a rival business. This the Company knew and feared. He was an officer who ruled with wisdom and authority, and his subordinate officers loved and respected him. Upon his retirement, he lived in Winnipeg, where, in collaboration with Charles Mair, he wrote his book, *Through the Mackenzie River Basin*.

MacFarlane was a great hand at arguing. Once at mess when he and Lockhart were discussing white foxes, Gaudet, who was a tease, began a discussion about the Pope of Rome. This was done to irritate MacFarlane, who jumped up from the table, declaring, "Gentlemen, I don't see the connection between the Pope of Rome and white foxes!"

He had a lot of little mannerisms. For instance, he hated milk and always took the cream off the jug for his porridge. Always there were two pitchers placed on the table, one with cream at

MacFarlane's end and the skimmed milk jug at the other. After saying grace, "Lord make us truly thankful for what we are about to receive," MacFarlane always lifted the pitcher and poured the cream on his own porridge.

The old chief factors who were in the country when I came ruled the Board. Chief Factor William McTavish was a great autocrat, though at times he lost his dignity. Once—he was inspector of the Eastern Fur District—he reported to Commissioner Wrigley at Fort Garry. Having indulged in perhaps a drink too many, he invited Chief Factor Belanger into his rig and had his coloured man drive them about the settlement. Finally, they went to a theatre where McTavish insisted on his coloured servant sitting between him and his guest. When the manager asked the Negro to take a back seat, McTavish indignantly refused to be separated from his man. His little sprees, however, did not interfere with his great ability as an officer.

Chief Factor James A. Grahame who, in 1874, became inspecting factor and subsequently senior officer of the British Columbia department of the Company, was an able officer, a good friend, but a bad enemy. In 1874 he quarrelled with Donald A. Smith over a land deal in British Columbia. Smith had the ear of the English Board. Grahame was retired from the Company with the sympathy of all the officers.

Chief Factor Herriot came to misfortune. He retired from the service and went to Montreal. There he took a great fancy to a smart young Company clerk named Wilson. He gave him all his money—between six and seven thousand pounds—to invest. I knew this Wilson well. He cleared out to the United States, and that was the last Herriot heard of his money. Sometime later, Roderick Ross, Herriot's son-in-law, discovered Wilson's whereabouts and tracked him down.

CHAPTER 15

I Return to Fort Rae

A fter an absence of some years, I returned to Fort Rae, where I remained in charge until the summer of 1883. I had been able while at this post to provide all the deer and caribou meat required for the brigades, but the clerk who succeeded me hadn't been able to secure more than half a boat-load of provisions. At Fort Rae we provided great quantities of provisions for the transports, keeping around three thousand pounds of dried meat stored on our shelves.

My transfer to St. John had come when the deer and caribou were changing their passes. As luck would have it, I returned to Fort Rae at the time the herds were shifting back to their feeding grounds and I was able to get three boatloads of provisions almost immediately—all that the brigades required. My trade in furs increased, too. It seemed that when I went to a new place, the volume of business increased. This was due to circumstances, but it helped my prestige.

Business was always good at Fort Rae. We took in, during an average year, the following:

One hundred bags of pemmican—one hundred pounds each
One hundred bales of dried meat—one hundred pounds each
One thousand pounds of tallow
Twelve hundred caribou tongues, salted, pickled, or smoked

and hung in groups of four
Fifteen bales of caribou skins
Three bales of babiche—forty to fifty skins in a bale

All skins were sorted. For the local trade (other posts) the bales consisted of deerskins, robes, and capotes. For the London market, the skins were assorted and packed separately. We usually sent a few good specimens of caribou heads to London. They were a curiosity there.

Donald A. Smith once sent to me for a good caribou head for Silver Heights, his place in Winnipeg. Occasionally the Company ordered a head for a museum. Fort Rae was really the center of a vast fur country. We collected all sorts of furs here and our average fur returns were between eight thousand and nine thousand dollars a year, even when low prices prevailed. The provisions and leather we provided for Fort Simpson paid the expenses of the post, leaving the profit on furs almost clear.

The Indians around the Fort Rae post made their tents out of moose skins, the Dogribs used deerskin, the Swampies favoured birch bark. Each tribe used the skins or materials native to its particular territory. The skins were laid on the ground and seamed like a sheet—sewn into long strips the height required for the tent—then laid over and around the raised tent poles. An opening was left at the top to allow smoke to escape. Some of the bands were beginning to buy six-ounce duck for tents.

Spring was the time for making pemmican. We made eight or nine hundred pounds at a time. The women made a big fire and melted the fat in large boat kettles, then poured it over the chopped, pounded meat, which was also in big kettles or piled on rawhides spread on the ground, mixing it thoroughly. This was expert work. The temperature of the fat had to be below boiling. Pemmican was packed very tightly in rawhide boxes or bags and pounded down with a mallet. We had special pemmican boxes made for packing the meat—about three feet long and two feet wide and they held one hundred pounds each. After the pemmican was taken out, the sides of the mixing kettles were scraped and these scrapings, or coarser bits, were given to the men for rations. After the bags were sewn up, they were turned from side to side every hour until they became thoroughly cool. This prevented the fat from setting on one side. We never put pemmican in storage until it was perfectly cold.

We generally made from seventy-five to one hundred bags at a time. The component parts were sixty-five parts meat, thirty-five parts grease. Everything was weighed before mixing. We made three kinds of pemmican: fine pemmican; common pemmican, and dog pemmican. For the fine pemmican we strained the grease through strips of cheesecloth. Into this finely pounded mixture we put raisins, berries, and a little salt. We made about fifty or sixty pounds of fine pemmican for the officers. Sometimes we sent Donald A. Smith a bag of fine pemmican for himself and his friends. Ordinary pemmican for freighters we did not make so carefully. The lumps strained from grease we used with cut, instead of pounded, meat for making dog pemmican. We used a saw to cut pemmican, to prevent waste. There was no extravagance in food in those days. Often hungry men would eat our dog pemmican, so to prevent this we put a little coal oil into it. The hungry dogs did not mind. Some years later when I was stationed at Fort Pelly, we made bannocks for the dogs out of oatmeal and small fish and treated them with coal oil.

Each tribe had its own method of trapping. An Indian trapper became an expert at his business, as he knew that undamaged furs would bring good prices while the poor ones fetched less.

While I was at Fort Rae, I entertained Captain H. P. Dawson, of the Polar Expedition, who came with three sergeants to make scientific observations. The party came with the Red River brigade from Fort Garry, then by team from Prince Albert to Ile-à-la-Crosse, thence by boat across Beaver River and Buffalo Lake to Portage La Loche, down to Fort Resolution, and on to Fort Rae.

I was on my way to England in August when I met the Dawson party coming up. Hardisty requested me to take them back to Fort Rae in the Fort Rae boat and I did. When we reached Fort Resolution, the brigades separated. Dawson's stuff—about six or eight tons—Dawson, his three sergeants, my wife and boy, and I would have to transfer to a York boat and this would overload it. "The thing is impossible. The boat cannot take such a load," I told Hardisty. He laughed and said, "Oh, you'll manage, King!" Hardisty always trusted me to manage, as I generally got through somehow, though it was often hard on me.

"By George," I said, "if we overload our boat, we'll all get drowned."

He said again, "You'll manage, King."

We got started from Fort Resolution on our journey about seven o'clock in the evening. Out in the channel between Moose Island and the shore, opposite the mouth of the river, about four miles out at sea, there is another island. By the time we reached this island it was blowing a stiff gale. The sea here, where the waves met the current from the river, was running high, but despite shipping a great deal of water, we managed to make the island. As the sun went down, around nine o'clock, we decided to camp. My men threw up my tent for myself and my family. Captain Dawson's men put up his tent and their own.

We hauled the boat to what we thought was a safe position, but in the night the wind altered, and the waves, coming into the bay that had been sheltered when we beached the boat, shifted its position, bouncing it against the stones. The guide, Jack Berens, was asleep in the boat, but the thumping wakened him. He sprang up and tore the cargo away to discover a large hole stove in the bottom. He gave a whooping call and all hands were soon on duty unloading the cargo. I gave my men orders to unload Dawson's stuff first. He had valuable scientific instruments. We then saved our gunpowder and cases of tea. After rescuing our cargo, we hauled the boat up and waited for daylight. Examination disclosed two large holes stove in the bottom.

We hadn't material to mend the boat properly, but the guide patched it up as well as he could, then took it back to Fort Resolution for the carpenter to put in a new plank. This delayed us a day. I decided now to put only the Fort Rae cargo on the boat. Dawson, hearing my order, looked pretty glum, but he cheered up when he heard me direct my men to take my cargo back to Fort Resolution, then come back for his. I sent directions to the clerk at Fort Resolution to examine my stuff and dry out what was wet.

I got the Dawson party and their luggage, my own family and boat crew, and about half a dozen pieces of my own cargo aboard and put off. We had to make a traverse to cut across the mouth of the river. It was late in the season and very stormy, and it was all we could do to get past the great sea, which was hard to navigate with even a half load. However, we got safely to Fort Rae and I sent the boat back to fetch my own cargo.

I took Dawson to live in my own house. John Hope, my assistant, put his wife and family in the garret and took the three sergeants into his house. Dawson and his party were at my post from August, when they began to make observations, until October first. I let them use the lot of dry timber I had ready to build a store to construct two observatories. They constructed the roofs of these observatories so they could be lifted to observe the stars.

Dawson had thermometers set everywhere—over water, under ice, on tops of mountains, in rivers, and on roofs of houses. He had about fifty different kinds of thermometers and scientific instruments. His work was very interesting and created great diversion at the fort. I had to have a fence put around his buildings to protect them from curious Indians and dogs.

At first the post Indians were greatly alarmed at Dawson's activities, as they thought he might be engaged in bringing about the end of the world. It required considerable tact to manage and keep them from running away. However, when they got used to Dawson's queer doings with instruments, which he occasionally let them look through, they were highly amused. He soon became a hero in their eyes.

One day Dawson saw a young Indian girl try to climb the stand where his tripod was set. He dashed out in time to give her a crack that sent her flying and save his instrument from disturbance. This was the only time I ever saw Dawson excited. He was apologetic about having given the girl such a crack, but I don't think he was very sorry. He found it difficult to keep curious Indians away.

Dawson was busy all the time. He had to read his thermometers daily. Sometimes dogs pulled away the canvases upon which he had set his thermometers, breaking them. He had many disturbances.

The sergeants entertained themselves by putting the Indians through all forms of military drill. On Sundays, Dawson and his men always attended fort service in full military uniform. This delighted the Indians. The Crees and Dogribs called the officers *Kitchie-hugo-moo-oaisis*, (the Queen's children). This was Cree. Then they began calling them *Chee-ma-ga-nees* (soldiers or fighting servants). The Indian boys around the fort learned to blow the bugle and by the time Dawson left, the Dogrib boys were walking in as good military fashion as the sergeants.

During Dawson's stay at Fort Rae there were, in addition to my family and John Hope and his family, John Garton, the teacher, who later became a minister, and also Robert Norme, fisherman for the fort, six engaged servants, and some temporary servants. Dawson's men gave the bugle call every morning, noon, and evening. This was not official, but it was very interesting.

Father Roure (who was afterwards killed by the Indians and his liver eaten) gave a dinner to honour Captain Dawson and Père Clut, the Roman Catholic bishop of the Mackenzie River District, who was his guest. Bishop Bompas was visiting the fort at the time and he was invited, but he did not attend. Dawson, the pleasantest fellow possible though the greatest scientist in the British army, was delighted. Père Roure's menu was baked porcupine, "to introduce Dawson to the fare of the country," he said. To get even with Père Roure, we invited him to a dinner of roasted muskrats stuffed with onions. We asked Bishop Bompas to say grace and Bishop Clut to give thanks. That *was* a merry dinner! Men of fine taste and appreciation all.

When he left, Dawson made me promise to visit him when I should go later to England. When I did call him up from London, he said, "I'll be up in the morning. Tell Mrs. King that we'll boil the kettle in Regent Street." This meant lunch. You have no idea how pleased I felt to have him remember our good native phrases. We stayed with him, at his home near Winchester, for a week and thoroughly enjoyed our visit. Mrs. Dawson greeted us with great warmth.

CHAPTER 16

Tale of a Cannibal

It was about a month after I left Fort Chipewyan that an Iroquois half-breed lay brother attached to Père Laity's mission at Chipewyan was reported to have eaten a lay brother and an Indian girl. We shall call him Louis.

He was an objectionable beggar—very cheeky. He had had his feet severely frozen at one time; this injury left him with a bad limp. He used to come to the post and bully and threaten our younger clerk. One day he came with an order from the mission. We were all in the house. I decided to fix him. I said to MacFarlane, "I'll not send the clerk, I'll go myself."

Inside the shop, this fellow began making his usual fuss. If I showed him this, he wanted that. Nothing pleased him. "Look here," I said, "I am not the clerk. If things don't suit you, get out or, lay brother or no lay brother, I'll kick you out!" He challenged me to a fight. I was going to be married in two weeks and didn't want to be scratched up, but I jumped over the counter, caught him, and threw him out the door. He ran, but I caught him. He kicked and scratched. I gave him a sound beating.

Père Laity was an awfully fine fellow. He had been in the French army. He was a great musician—a fine drummer. When Louis returned to the mission with black eyes and without goods, he came to inquire into the affair. MacFarlane said, "You had better speak to King!" When I told the père about Louis's tricks with our clerk and my decision to teach him a lesson, he fairly split his sides laughing. He said, "I hope 'twill do him good." No doubt he, too, had had trouble with the beggar.

Père Laity also had charge of the Catholic mission at Lac La Biche. He had two boats for carrying supplies between the two posts. In September when his two good boatmen were late returning from a hunt, he decided to send Louis with another lay brother and some Indian boys with the boats. He sent, as passenger, a native girl that he was transferring from the Chipewyan convent school to Lac La Biche.

It was a bad time of year—the time of autumn storms. Cold weather overtook the travellers. They were delayed by ice and, not being expert boatmen, their boats got caught in the rapids and frozen in. Louis sent the men back overland to Fort Chipewyan. He said he would go forward to Lac La Biche on foot with the other brother and the girl. He had a few provisions and a gun.

Word finally reached Père Laity that Louis and his party had not reached their destination. Indian search parties were immediately sent out from both mission stations. They met an Indian moose hunter who had discovered tracks from the boat to a trail. He had not followed them, he said, but had reported the matter to Isaac Cowie, who was at Fort McMurray at that time. Indians can read camp signs like a book. They followed the trail and discovered where three had camped and slept, then two, and finally only one. They found no signs of food. They concluded that Louis had eaten his companions. They had found the clothes and bones of his victims on the trail.

The Indians believed that a person who had eaten human flesh was transformed into a *weettako*—a human devil. They were terrified. Louis was found and shot by a Wood Cree Indian. This was not a Company matter. Such things happened in the North.

The post at Lac La Biche[11] was built by Peter Fidler in 1798, when he wintered there. He called La Biche River the Red Deer River. The Hudson's Bay Company took it over after the coalition of 1821. It was raided by Indians in the 1885 rebellion.

The original Chipewyan post was built by Peter Pond in 1778 on Athabaska River, about thirty miles above the outlet on the west side. At that time, Athabaska River and Lake were called Elk River and Lake of the Hills. It was also called Athabaska (meeting place of many waters), Old Establishment, and Pond's House.

The site of the post was twice changed by the North West Company. One was built by Roderick Mackenzie on a rocky point which ran into the lake. It was called Emporium of the North and Little Athens of the Hyperborean Regions. In 1804 a fort, the present one, was put up. It was the most important North West Company fort in the far north. The Hudson's Bay Company took it over in 1821.

We had fine buildings—eight houses for the employees; a clerk's house, forty by thirty by seventeen feet, well plastered and warm; and a fine factor's house. We had a large general store, sixty-three by thirty-one by seventeen feet, near the landing. When Professor Macoun came to my post he was amused because it had such a large glass window. We kept our buildings here, as at all posts, in good repair and whitewashed.

I remember a trip which I took over Great Slave Lake in the year 1876. Mr. Andrew Flett, who was temporarily in charge of Fort Rae, and his family, I and my family, and Reverend Mr. Reeve were coming up Mackenzie's river. The boat was overloaded. This was not dangerous in calm weather, but in autumn storms it was thoroughly unsafe.

When we got to Big Island, we found it impossible to take the cargo and all the passengers further. I left my wife and son at Fort Providence. Mr. Flett also left his family there. We decided to risk Mr. Reeve. Still, we were overloaded. We had bad weather for three days but managed to get through. The steersman refused to go out to sea in the lake, but we had in the crew an old Orkney seaman who had gone whale fishing in the Arctic. He said he would steer, and he took us safely through the storm. Then we met head winds. We had to take a chance on running ashore into a bay. There was no beach—only a rocky shore. We got our cargo unloaded and the boat hauled up, as we thought, safely.

During the night the wind altered and a terrific storm came up. We worked all night trying to save the boat. Trees fell around us, and some of the men narrowly escaped severe injury. In spite of our efforts, the boat was smashed to pieces against the rocks. It was a complete wreck—beyond repair. We were obliged to cache our cargo and walk across land to Fort Rae—a distance of 120 miles.

We were not prepared with winter clothes. We had only a few bannocks. The walking was bad. There was snow on the ground and we sank in the swamps, which were not completely frozen. But our Indian boatmen were excellent guides. They knew where to avoid lakes and shorten the distance. We shot a moose and got on. The ice which we had to cross to reach Fort Rae was extremely thin. The Indians separated from us as we neared the post, which is on a point. Mrs. Reeve came down from her house to meet her husband. He was fifty yards from the shore and very weak. We warned him not to attempt the brittle ice, but he struck out, broke through, and managed to reach the shore. His wife threw her arms around him, calling him "dear William" over and over. Dear William was soaking wet.

This year a party of Dogrib hunters went to the west side of Great Slave Lake and Fort Providence. This was a great hunting territory of 120 miles. Deer wintered here in great herds. An old hunter, called Pot Fighter, went with them. Old Pot Fighter decided to go on a little hunt of his own. He told the women that he would be only one night away. This meant a two-day trip. When he did not return promptly, the young hunters went in search of him. They found him dead between his fire and his little camp. His scalp was practically torn off and his hands were bitten. His gun was lying in the snow. He had been attacked, the hunters saw, by a wolf. A wolf had been bothering them. The old hunter had sat asleep beside his dead fire when he was attacked and killed. In his hands were bunches of wolf hair and wolf hair lay all about.

The young hunters decided to get the wolf, no matter how long it took. When they returned to camp another hunter reported that a wolf had tried to attack him. It was not usual for wolves to attack hunters when deer were plentiful, or at any time, unless they were starving. The hunters finally tracked the wolf to his den and shot him. They found shreds of Pot Fighter's clothes in his claws.

Another time at the fort two little Indian girls went out with their father to pile wood as he cut it—about two miles from the post. The father left the girls behind with their sled to bring the wood back. On their way they saw two wolves watching them. Thoroughly frightened, they went back to their fire and built it up. Wolves will not approach a good fire. Night came and it grew cold. The wolves came nearer. The girls, twelve and fourteen respectively, climbed the trees and fastened themselves to the branches with their sinew ropes. The wolves crept to the dying camp fire. All night they stayed there watching the girls, who never stopped calling in the hope that someone near the fort might hear. When the girls did not come home, their father thought they had gone to spend the night in a neighbouring tent. In the morning, he went in search of them. He found them in the trees, almost frozen. Two wolves were sitting beside the dead camp fire. He shot them both.[12]

CHAPTER 17

From Fort Smith
to York Factory

O n July 13, 1883, I assumed charge of Fort Smith in the
Athabaska District. The Athabaska and Mackenzie river
boats came here to what we called the Mountain Portage,
and it was my duty, in addition to looking after the post, to super-
vise the transportation of all cargoes back and forth across this
sixteen-mile portage. I was provided with twelve old oxen, ten
Red River carts, one very elderly man, named Clarke, and a young
man, named Vincent—a poor working outfit. This cart transport
had started the year before.

The ten carts made on an average about five full trips a week,
each cart carrying, each way, from 600 to 800 pounds. I planned a
trip a day for each cart, barring accidents. This queer outfit was
unfit to carry heavy loads. In four months, however, we hauled
about 6,400 pounds. In a full season we could haul from 8,000 to
10,000 pounds. Half of this cargo was furs going out; the other,
merchandise coming in. When MacFarlane arrived from
Athabaska he was surprised at the amount of work we had been
able to handle with this poorly equipped transport.

The salt springs were near the fort and they attracted deer and
many other animals, so consequently it was a good fur country.

We had fine Chipewyan and Montagnais Indian hunters in the region and at the post. Old Beaulieu's tribe brought us valuable furs.

Owing to the nature of the country, the furs around Fort Smith were of fine quality. Except at Fort Liard, very few fishers were traded. There were no snakes in this part of the country. No snakes, badgers, or skunks were ever found in the region north of the Salt River approaching Mackenzie's river and the Arctic. Only after the country became civilized, opened up to farming, did these animals penetrate into the North.

The year after I left Fort Smith, the priest Père Enard, and his brother were drowned. They overbalanced their canoe while setting a net. Both bodies were caught and trapped in the net.

When I left Fort Smith, I sold my dog team and harness for twenty pounds, which was very cheap. It was the best dog team in the district. But I still had Fancy, the mother, who was devoted to, and guarded, my son.

Fancy used to sleep beside the boy's bed. One evening she was missing. The lad got dressed and went out to the fort gate, and under some freighting carts he saw the green light from Fancy's eyes. She was injured and came to him, panting. The boy began to cry and ran for me. It turned out that she had beaten a dog belonging to an Indian woman—Fancy was boss of the dogs—and the woman had stabbed her.

I went to the woman's house. She confessed that she had stabbed Fancy. In a rage, I said, to scare her, "You will die soon!" I was surprised when my prophecy came true. The woman died within a few months. The Indians were now sure that I had put a spell on her. They had additional respect for me after that and were pretty careful how they behaved.

On her return from England once, Mrs. Bompas brought two good pups: a female retriever and a Scotch staghound. She wanted to breed these dogs to cross with the dogs of the country in order to get a good dog team for her husband. The idea was to get dogs with good hair and hard feet. From this crossbreeding with huskies I had got Fancy as a pup from Mrs. Bompas for my boy.

During the early part of trading season 1884, I went to England on a furlough. My business was mostly to leave my son in school. My family, the Kings, are lineal descendants of William of

Wykeham, who established Winchester College. In the original charter it was set out that all his descendants would be permitted to attend this school free of charge and that they would be provided with clothes. I thought of putting my son in this school. I found when I got to England that this charter had been outlawed. The name of a King, my uncle, appears in the records of this school.

While at home, Sir Richard King, the head of our family, gave a family dinner in my honour. My uncle, Admiral George King, said, "Rats, I hear you've saved some money. No King ever saved money, even on a large income. What is your salary?"

When I told him that my first contract was for twenty-five pounds a year, he said, "How could you have saved money on that? I am giving a family dinner for you next week. Bring your bank account along. For every pound you've saved, I'll match it with a pound."

The day of the admiral's dinner came. After dinner, we sat around smoking. After a bit, Uncle George asked, "About this account, Rats?" I tried to look modest and handed him my bank account. I had saved 117 pounds, some shillings, and pence.

"Well, well!" he said, shaking his head and handing the account to the other members of the family.

When I was leaving he handed me an envelope containing a draft for 120 pounds. When I presented this cheque at the bank, the clerk refused to honour it. It was a crossed cheque, which could be cashed only through a business firm. I asked to see President Charles Barnett, who was a relative. He arranged to let me have the money without waiting for the cheque to go through in the regular way.

On my way to England, I had come across Riel at Prince Albert. Chief Factor Lawrence Clarke, who was in charge of the Prince Albert trading post, invited me to look in at a meeting of the patriots that Riel was holding. We found Riel addressing a large meeting of the plainsmen. He was a fiery speaker and his oration about the rights of his people was masterly. He spoke in English, French, and Cree.

When the meeting was over, he came to me and presented his views. I said, "You're talking rot! Start a rumpus and you will be destroyed."

He became very indignant. "What right have you, a Hudson's

Bay Company man, to tell me, Louis Riel, what the *rights* of my people are?" he asked.

I refused to argue with him.

When I visited the office of the Company in London, Ware, the secretary, laughed about the idea of the half-breeds starting a rebellion in the country, as the London people called it. "The Company is powerful enough to put down an uprising," he said.

"Don't be too confident," I warned him. "Conditions in the country are changing and, right or wrong, Riel is a clever, well-educated man of the country and a leader. Many of the Métis people possess sound judgment. They are strong and they are ready for trouble."

Ware laughed. His attitude was that the London directors knew more about conditions in the country than those of us who lived and worked in it.

The rebellion broke out before I left London. Ware was greatly surprised. This year, 1884, I was promoted to the rank of junior chief trader.

When I refused the offers of my people to quit the Company and return to England on a remittance, Sir Richard King, the head of the family, said, "Rats has got his tail up! He'll see the thing through!"

To be candid, apart from the obvious unfairness of some of the ruling factors, I felt a pride in the Company. I was a wintering partner.

In 1885, on my return from England, I went to Ile-à-la-Crosse under Chief Factor Joseph Fortescue. On the boat with me from Fort Garry were Camsell, also on his way back from England, Archibald McDougall and his wife and child, and Mr. Fortescue and his wife. At Fort à la Corne, we met the steamer *North-West* coming down with a brigade of soldiers returning from the Riel Rebellion. Big Bear had been captured. These barges came along-side our steamer to get the mail, and the officers of both outfits chatted together for a while. The soldiers, seeing me leaning over the side of the boat, asked me if I had anything to drink. I had a case of rum, so I handed the fellows a couple of bottles.

A day or two later we arrived at the Prince Albert post. Chief Factor Lawrence Clarke, who was in charge, provided us with teams and drivers, one named La Roque. Mr. and Mrs. Fortescue and my wife and I travelled in one democrat. The roads were pretty rough. Fortescue grew tired of the bumping and went ahead and sat on the freighters' wagon with La Roque. He kept grumbling about the damned roads. Finally La Roque said, in broken English, "Good for the liver, Mr. Fortescue!" Ordinarily this would have amused Fortescue, but to our amusement he grew indignant. The corduroy roads had completely upset him.

We shot a couple of Strong Wood deer as we went along. They were very beautiful animals with fine antlers. At the south end of Green Lake, we got aboard the Ile-à-la-Crosse boats. As soon as he touched water, travelling in old style, Fortescue recovered his temper. The Cree crew were fine boatmen and we went smoothly over the water to the Green Lake post. It took us three days to make the trip. Just after we passed over the Green Lake trail the mail was held up and robbed.

Mrs. Fortescue could speak Cree. Born at York Factory, she was the daughter of Reverend Mr. Mason and Mrs. Mason. She and I were old friends; we had come from England together. She was then on her way home from school; I, on my way to the country.

As district manager, Mr. Fortescue did not get on very agreeably with the Indians. As soon as we reached the post, we found Indian traders waiting to interview him. The meeting was unsatisfactory. Fortescue said to me, "I am going to keep you here! I am head of this district and this post. I want you to carry on the business and the trading for me. Nominally, you will be trading manager." I didn't wish to stay at this post as second officer. MacFarlane wanted me back at Chipewyan and that was my choice also, but Fortescue overruled my objections, saying that he would arrange everything with MacFarlane. He wrote MacFarlane praising me. I was grateful but not pleased. MacFarlane was displeased about my transfer.

Mr. Fortescue soon got at loggerheads with Père Rapport, a very nice man, whom he accused of interfering with the religion of the Indians. The whole affair started over a church holy day. Père Rapport told the Indians and the Métis people that they were obliged to keep a feast day. It was spring and Fortescue had arranged for the boats to start for Green Lake on the feast day.

The boatmen explained their position in regard to their command to go to church. Fortescue insisted that the trip must be made, and rightly. He spoke to Père Rapport, accusing him of upsetting the business of the Company. Père Rapport declared that he was not interfering with the men, saying that he had merely told them that this day was an important church holy day, though it was not compulsory for them to give up work. Fortescue insisted on the brigade leaving for Green Lake at the scheduled time. The men refused to go until the next day.

I advised Fortescue to wait. I argued that if the men went away sulky and resentful, they would make no effort to land the cargo on time. If they went agreeably, they would—even if a day late in starting—try to make up time. These men, I said, had pride in their skill as boatmen and in keeping up their record. Fortescue insisted that when he gave an order it must be obeyed.

The time came for the brigade to start. Not a man appeared! I went to the Indian crew and said, "In the middle of the night, when your holy day is over, I want you to start!" Every man appeared at the appointed time. I got them off.

Fortescue got in a huff because the boatmen had listened to me and not to him, but he didn't say much. I assured him that the boatmen would make the portage on time. They did and Forestcue's good humour was restored. Fortescue was a splendid office man; he wrote wonderful letters and reports. His only fault was that he was inclined to make mountains out of molehills. He was used to the old kind of Hudson's Bay authority. He was a great officer, but a very poor trader.

Ile-à -la Crosse was an interesting place. Frobisher was in the vicinity in 1776; David Thompson, the great geographer, in 1804; and Harmon, of Andover, Massachusetts, in 1808.

Upon instructions from Commissioner Joseph Wrigley, I proceeded, in 1886, to take charge of Fort Pelly in the Swan River District. Civilization was creeping in here. I witnessed the first annual treaty payment to the Indians in the district. Commissioner Wrigley came from Fort Garry with the treaty party; he was accompanied by Chief Factor Archibald McDonald of the Swan River District. In addressing the Indians, Wrigley praised the Company and the government for what they were doing for the Indian people. He advised them to love the Queen.

Chief Cote of the Crowstand reserve, Ke-ze-kouse, chief of the Salteaux, and George Brass, chief of the Swampy Crees, were present. The people of the combined tribes numbered between two hundred and three hundred.

The meeting began badly. The commissioner kept his gloves on when he greeted the chiefs. Cote threw back Wrigley's hand, saying that he never shook hands with a gloved man. The Indians believed that only bare hands should be clasped in friendship. Chief Cote rose and said,"I do not love the Queen. How can I? She took our country and gave us a little bacon and five dollars a year. She shut us away on reserves like wild animals. If we went to your country and did the same to you, would you love us? If our people were strong enough we would drive the white men out of the country at once."

McDonald interpreted Cote's speech to the commissioner. It took considerable tact to handle Cote and that treaty payment successfully.

I shall always remember how Cote looked as he stood before Wrigley, tall and dignified. He was one of the greatest warriors of the plains, a pure Indian. His dealings with the Company were honourable and he was a man of his word.

Wrigley came really to see about the tariff. The country was changing fast. People were becoming educated. The Company was abandoning the made beaver valuation. It was also abandoning the pounds, shillings, and pence currency and beginning to trade in dollars and cents. The commissioner was on his way through the Southern Fur District, changing this system. The introduction of dollars and cents marked the change in the old, recognized forms of currency in the Company's dealings with the Indians and also in our accounts. A made beaver valuation went thus:

Article	Made Beaver
1 Gun	12
1 lb. Powder	2
4 lbs. Shot	1
1 Hatchet	$\frac{1}{8}$
1 Knife	$\frac{1}{8}$
1 Red Coat	5
1 lb. Tobacco	5

In my first year at Fort Pelly I collected pelts to the value of eight thousand dollars; the next year, between nine thousand and ten thousand dollars. We got lynx there in thousands. Lynx and bear were the principal furs, although we collected all sorts of mixed furs. The best bearskins in the country, black and brown, were collected at this post. A bearskin was valued up to ten or twelve made beaver. Nominally, a beaver skin was valued at two or three made beaver, according to its size, quality, and location. This too was a wonderful muskrat country. Prices now began to go up.

Fort Pelly was a well-built post, sheltered on the north by woods. It was built on the east side of the Assiniboine River, on sandy ground. It was protected by a stout, high wall of sawn planks. From 1806, Fort Pelly was one of the main trading posts of the Company. Boats of three to four tons capacity came down the Swan River annually, taking cargoes of furs to York Factory. This enabled the Company to trade goods with the Indians a month earlier than the North West Company, whose goods were transported from Montreal to Fort William and thence distributed. A short portage led from Fort Pelly to the Swan River. Fort Pelly was operated by the Hudson's Bay Company for over one hundred years—until about 1900.

From Fort Pelly I went to Moose Lake, where I stayed in charge from 1889 to 1894, until I went to England. On my return I went to Cedar Lake. Tyrrell, who was travelling for the government, came down to Cedar Lake. I was interested in amber and showed him the piece a boatman had picked up some twenty years earlier. I had first seen amber in this region in 1863, when I came to the country, but had forgotten completely about it until Tyrrell became interested.

We walked down to the beach to look at the amber deposit, which lay under the debris of rotten wood, and threaded off from a thickness of two feet at the water's edge to nothing. Tyrrell began at once to figure how much there was in this particular deposit and estimated there were tons of it in this spot. He sent a report of it to the government and to the papers.

In the evening he got out maps. "Look here," I said. "You are a scientific fellow. Why don't you follow in the footsteps of Dr. Rae and make new discoveries?" I suggested a route that he might take. A year later I heard that he had started from the point and over the route I had suggested, taking with him Corrigal, the good man I recommended. Corrigal had accompanied Sir John Franklin and had also been a guide with Dr. John Rae.

A year later I received a pleasant letter from Tyrrell thanking me for the information I had given him, which had started him off.

He promised to see me later. When next I saw Corrigal, he told me about Tyrrell's trip. He proved a valuable guide for Tyrrell. Corrigal had been at Ile-à-la-Crosse with me and he used to accompany me on trips. He was a Red River Métis and most reliable. He died not many years ago at Selkirk, Manitoba. Corrigal told me that he had gone to York Factory, with half a dozen other Red River men, to meet Dr. Rae and guide him on his exploratory trips. I knew that he had been Dr. Rae's right-hand man. He often told me that he had never seen such a traveller as Dr. Rae, who had, in going over country which he or no other man had ever travelled, not only led the party but also provided most of the game.

I had charge of York Factory during 1900-01. This was an important depot, with seven posts attached to it, extending from Weenusk River to Island Lake to God's Lake. These outposts had flying posts attached to them, which were kept up in winter only. My rank was chief trader. My annual fur returns from this district were from thirty thousand to forty thousand dollars a year, so you can see my luck in collecting furs continued here.

Foxes came along the shore of the bay and its rivers in great numbers. Normally only two or three hundred foxes were taken here in a year. We had an unusual migration of marten, too, and as the harbour was shallow (land level), whales were often washed ashore.

I had a reserve supply of traps—six or eight cases of traps, two or three dozen to a case. I gave the hunters a dozen traps each instead of the usual two or three, on the condition that they would bring to my post every fur they caught. I sent ten of my best engaged servants out amongst the Indians to buy furs. The white fox pelts were worth six shillings each at Fort Garry and they sold in England for eight dollars to ten dollars apiece. I got more than two thousand white fox pelts. I did not get many beaver skins. The beavers preferred fresh rather than brackish water.

The opening of the country to agriculture in late years, however, has driven the beaver to the coast, all through the district, back a little from the sea. Salt and brackish water affects the quality of beaver fur. There were plenty of white and polar bears—no black or brown—within fifty miles of the post.

Life at York Factory was semi-civilized. We were in closer

touch with England, by contact with the ships, than any of the Company posts. I was also custom's officer while I was at York and the government allowed me three hundred dollars a year for this work.

I spent the winter of 1901-02 in the Keewatin District. This was my last winter of active service. I retired from the Company, officially, on June 1, 1903.

The romance of the fur trade is dead. Now that the personal element has been removed, the fur business has become mechanical like other businesses. Men no longer seek adventure. Importing trading supplies in the old days was a matter of life and death. Supplies and transportation facilities were limited and every man worked as a matter of pride and to the best of his ability. It was pride in achievement, the overcoming of obstacles that spurred a man on.

I was considered a bit of a rebel by the chief factors, but a servant had to use judgment and discretion in his decisions. Every man in the service wanted results. He wanted to be valuable to the Company. It was—and quite right—dangerous and an offence for one to depart from the strict rules laid down by the Board. The Board gave orders to the commissioner; the district managers, in turn, gave orders to the post managers.

When I was in charge of a post, if orders were good, I carried them out. If not, I handled them in my own way. I was willing to be judged by results. Sometimes the orders from England were absolutely idiotic. All right for London, perhaps, but no good in the Mackenzie River District fur trade. I did not look for credit for myself. If my own decisions brought the desired results, I let the honour go to the district manager. We were above money consideration. We were the Company.

I often recall my experiences and I should enjoy living them over again. Often I have gone through the ashes of my campfire for scraps I had thrown away. I have had many hardships, but I have not complained. None of the men that I knew—and they included all ranks in the service who carried on the enormous business of the Company in the far North—complained. I have gone from apprentice clerk to district manager to supervisor of posts. I have given my life to the service of the Company: forty years of active duty, nine years retirement, three years full pay, six years half pay, and now the Company gives me a grant of ninety pounds a year. I am one of the last pensioned commissioned officers. The governors of the Hudson's Bay Company come to see me when they visit Canada. I belong to the old brigade.

CHAPTER 18

Trader King's Account of the Last Council Meeting

We come now to the year of 1896, the year of the last great council meeting. At Fort Garry that year, Commissioner Joseph Wrigley gave a dinner for the commissioned officers and their wives. At that time the commissioner's house was on Garry Street, between Broadway and Assiniboine Avenue. Commissioner C. C. Chipman lived there winters for a number of years; in summer he took his family to Lower Fort Garry.

The last Hudson Bay Company council meeting (1896-97) was held at Athabaska Landing, North West Territories.

Object: Canada was growing fast, the population increasing, means of communication and transport improving, especially to the North-West. These changes impelled the Company to reorganize their methods of business to the requirements of the day.

Instructions were issued by the London Board to C. C. Chipman, the Canadian commissioner at Winnipeg, to call a meeting of the officers. For convenience of the northern officers, Athabaska Landing, north of Edmonton was chosen. Five other northern district officers and I were directed to meet Commissioner C. C. Chipman and the Winnipeg staff on a certain date at an appointed place.

I joined the party at Regina and we started for Edmonton. Miss Flora Shaw, a protégé of Lord Strathcona, accompanied Commissioner Chipman and his party. She was gathering material for a book. We all arrived on time.

From Edmonton to Athabaska Landing, all transport and travelling arrangements were made for the party, including tents, bedding, food, servants, two democrats, and a wagon (all complete).

We spent two busy and enjoyable days at Edmonton. Commissioner Chipman and Miss Shaw and the secretaries were guests at one hotel; C. F. McDougal, E. R. Beeston, John Calder and I were at the other. Our evenings were free to spend as we pleased.

We left Edmonton at 9:00 AM, planning to dine at noon at a place about twenty miles on our way. A local guide drove the commissioner's democrat, with passengers Mr. Chipman and Miss Shaw in the back seat and Mr. Mantel with the driver in front. Mr. W. Livock drove democrat number two, with Mr. C. F. McDougal, Beeston, and myself as passengers. A fret wagon with tents, baggage, food, official box (accounts), and documents accompanied us. We had a hired man, named Stern, to erect tents, to serve at mealtime, and to make himself generally useful. When we reached the appointed stopping place for mid-day lunch, Stern and all hands got busy. Miss Shaw sat at one end of the canvas spread on the ground, Mr. Chipman at the other end. The rest of the party sat within reach of the dishes set out.

After lunch we packed up and started. When we reached the halfway house it was full so we had to put up our tents. We built a campfire and had an evening singsong, led by Miss Shaw, who was about thirty and very jolly. She had been stenographer to Cecil Rhodes in Africa; she later married General Lasard of Bermuda.

At 9:00 AM the next morning we packed up and got underway, giving our fret wagon (with the food) an hour's start with orders to drive fast. This those in charge did, but we reached the noon stopping place before them, collected wood, made a fire, and put up a shelter for Miss Shaw. We drove through a terrible dust storm all the morning. Mr. Livock had supplied us all with nice, white dust storm coats, but they weren't much protection. That night we reached the Company's post at Athabaska Landing.

Mr. Chipman and Miss Shaw put up with Mr. and Mrs. Leslie Wood at the Company's house. Mr. and Mrs. Ewan McDonald put up their tent. The six northern fur trade officers, including myself, slept in another building, upstairs. Downstairs was the council room. We had our meals in Mr. Leslie Wood's house, with three women and a half-breed girl of seventeen attending us. This service was so slow that we waited on ourselves. Mr. E. McDonald said grace. Mr. Chipman said we were too long at meals. The ladies spoke up and said there was no rush—this settled matters. Miss Shaw was the life of the party. Mrs. Ewan McDonald acted as chaperone and Mrs. Wood supervised the cooking. Even Mr. Chipman thawed out. Evenings we had songs and dancing and half the village ladies came to our campfire and enjoyed themselves. The daily meetings were from 9:30 AM until noon and from 2:00 PM until 4:30. The business of the meeting was all arranged beforehand at Winnipeg. With the singing of "God Save the Queen" at midnight, the 1897 council meeting was dismissed.

On the return trip to Edmonton, we travelled again through heavy dust storms. We stopped at noon for a hurried meal. Mr. Chipman, Miss Shaw, Mantel, and the driver went on ahead—they had a better team than ours. We landed at Edmonton at 7:00 PM. The next day the official party started for Winnipeg; I left them at Calgary.

This council meeting authorized many necessary changes. Railroads and steamboats had displaced canoes, boats, ox carts, dog teams, and snowshoes, which, good in their day, had become obsolete. Fur tariff had to be revised in accordance with the prices of other traders and the stores. Money had to be used in trade in place of the made beaver system. The staff and employees of the Company had to be reduced. Boatmen were no longer needed. Provisions, to take the place of country produce such as buffalo, moose, deer, lynx, rabbit, etc., were imported.

Missionaries of many denominations, Indian agents, Mounted Police, travellers, prospectors, white trappers, fish companies, etc., were becoming established in the country. There was no longer inducement for the Indians to hunt for a living. They could get better pay at regular work. They could buy food. By 1900 the North-West was completely changed from the time of my arrival.

The last council meeting affected the following districts and managers:

Chief Factor J. S. Camsell
—Mackenzie River District (10 outposts)

Factor Dr. Wm. A. E. McKay
—Athabaska District (5 outposts)

Factor Ewan MacDonald
—Upper Peace River and Lesser Slave Lake (5 outposts)

Chief Trader Wm. C. King
—English River District (5 outposts)

Chief Factor Jas. McDougal
—Cumberland District (5 outposts)

Factor W. Livock
—Edmonton and North Sask. (6 outposts)

Winnipeg Staff: Commissioner C. C. Chipman and Secretary Mantel, G. Calder, chief accountant, Winnipeg office.

THE END

Appendix

Progression of promotion for fur-trading employees of the Hudson's Bay Company:

Postmaster; Clerk; Junior Chief Trader; Chief Trader; Factor; Chief Factor; Inspecting Chief Factor; Commissioner.
The Junior Chief Trader, Factor, Inspecting Chief Factor, and Commissioner were instituted after the new deed poll in 1871.

Note: It has been suggested by Clifford P. Wilson, editor of *The Beaver* magazine, that the expression Strong Wood deer refers to deer living in the thick woods as opposed to those who live on the prairies or in the "little sticks" on the edge of the Barrens. This expression probably comes from the French *bois fort*.

Notes to *Trader King*

1. Full name: The Governor and Company of Adventurers of England Trading into Hudson's Bay.

2. The muskrat push-ups or feeding lot is not usually regarded as a house. See "Ratting in the Delta," *The Beaver* magazine, March, 1948.

3. Order.

4. Fort Nelson was originally established by men of the North West Company in the early 1800s and named after the hero of Trafalgar. In the winter of 1812–13, it was attacked and the occupants murdered by the Indians. Several writers have stated that the celebrated Alexander Henry the younger was among the killed. Actually, he was drowned in 1814 at the mouth of the Columbia River. After the massacre, the fort lay deserted until re-established by W. Cornwallis King in 1865. Today it is one of the main depots along the Alaska Highway.

5. Father of Dr. Charles Camsell.

6. Laurence Clarke, writing to Chief Factor Jas. Anderson on February 26, 1856, describes Fort Rae as being distant about three

miles from the main shores of Great Slave Lake and adds that the fort was "situated on the western extremity of an island about 5x3 miles in extent, the most prominent and largest cluster which enfilades some miles within a deep bay or inlet to the N.E. end of Great Slave Lake." Clarke states that he found the buildings erected in outfit 1853 too crowded for the transaction of the business of the fort and says that he intended "to add another wing thereto (15x20 feet)."

7. The posts were different from the forts. The Company forts (in a strict sense) were Fort Garry, Lower Fort Garry, Fort Prince of Wales at Churchill, Fort Pelly, Fort Carlton, and Fort Edmonton. The posts were simply a collection of log houses—say, six buildings, flagstaff, well, powder magazine, wooden fur press, and a garden for vegetables, which might or might not have a fence around it to keep the dogs or horses in or out.

8. In 1863, when Mr. King went into the North, the name of Sir John Franklin was on the tongue of every Mackenzie River voyageur. Overland explorers were more or less in the hands of Company officers, who had to supply them with provisions, Indian guides, and hunters. The search for Franklin was still continuing, despite the fact that in 1853–54 Dr. John Rae, a Hudson's Bay factor, had brought from the North relics of the Franklin expedition which he had gathered from the Eskimo, and had been awarded the ten thousand pounds offered by the British Admiralty for definite news of Franklin's fate. At the posts there was a good deal of speculation about how much Franklin's expedition, and those sent in search of him, had accomplished in the way of exact geographical knowledge of a great area of hitherto unknown country, as well as the thousands of miles of coastline which they had discovered.

Mr. King's stories of this period in the fur trade form a direct link with the great age of exploration in the North-West. Franklin mentions a guide named Keskarrah, elder brother of Akaitcho (Chief Confidante) who traded at Fort Rae, who said he had accompanied Hearne to the Arctic. Keskoray, who was King's post hunter, may well have been a son or nephew to Chief Confidante.

9. This would be governor, deputy-governor, and committee, now called the governor and committee.

10. Harmon visited Hudson's Hope in 1810. He refers to it as Rocky Mountain Portage.

11. A Hudson's Bay post was opened there in 1947.

12. One day, some of the Indian women going back to pick berries saw on a traverse a great moose swimming. He had very large antlers. They followed him cautiously in their canoe. When they got near, they wet their blankets, ran the canoe right up on his back, threw the blankets over his head, and held it under water until he drowned. Then, tying a line to his antlers, they towed him ashore. There was no berry picking that day.

Introducing the Western Canadian Classics

F ifth House Publishers is pleased to present the Western Canadian Classics series, designed to keep the best western Canadian history, biography, and other works available in attractive and affordable editions. The popular and best-selling books are selected for their quality, enduring appeal, and importance to an understanding of our past.

Look for these Western Canadian Classics at your favourite bookstore.